T0072400

Answers from the Bible

A Bible Study Guide for the Confused, Unlearned, and Disoriented

By Seth Carl

Copyright 2000
Copyright 2013

AuthorHouse™ LLC
1663 Liberty Drive
Bloomington, IN 47403
www.authorhouse.com
Phone: 1-800-839-8640

© 2014 Seth Carl. All rights reserved.

*No part of this book may be reproduced, stored in a retrieval system, or transmitted
by any means without the written permission of the author.*

Published by AuthorHouse   08/14/2014

ISBN: 978-1-4969-3286-0 (sc)
ISBN: 978-1-4969-3461-1 (e)

*Any people depicted in stock imagery provided by Thinkstock are models,
and such images are being used for illustrative purposes only.
Certain stock imagery © Thinkstock.*

This book is printed on acid-free paper.

*Because of the dynamic nature of the Internet, any web addresses or links contained in this book may have changed
since publication and may no longer be valid. The views expressed in this work are solely those of the author and do
not necessarily reflect the views of the publisher, and the publisher hereby disclaims any responsibility for them.*

*This guide is based on four (4) versions of the Bible. The Authorized King James Version, The New King
James Version, The New American Standard Version, and The New International Version. But The Authorized
King James Version is never to be made obsolete. Many teachings are best understood with the A.K.J.V.*

*Topic names and key words in scripture references will match at least one of these versions, but not necessarily
all. But they will mean the same, but will use different names and words because of different contexts.*

*Besides trying to inspire people to start the habit of reading The Bible, this guide also tries to point out topics of
modern-day issues, such as Abortion, Bullying, Family Values, Marriage, Homosexuality, Creation, Evolution, . . .*

*Scripture quotations marked KJV are from the Holy Bible, King James Version (Authorized Version). First published
in 1611. Quoted from the KJV Classic Reference Bible, Copyright © 1983 by The Zondervan Corporation.*

*Scripture quotations marked NASB are taken from the New American Standard Bible®, Copyright © 1960,
1962, 1963, 1968, 1971, 1972, 1973, 1975, 1977, 1995 by The Lockman Foundation. Used by permission.*

*Scripture quotations marked NIV are taken from the Holy Bible, New International Version®. NIV®. Copyright ©
1973, 1978, 1984 by International Bible Society. Used by permission of Zondervan. All rights reserved. [Biblica]*

*Scripture quotations marked NKJV are taken from the New King James Version. Copyright
© 1982 by Thomas Nelson, Inc. Used by permission. All rights reserved.*

Preface

It is estimated that every year, 300,000 new books are published worldwide. What a torrent of print! Yet, one volume, the Bible, stands out above all others.

How do we explain the appeal of this ancient book? The answer is simple. It is Gods Word, given in human language, and it tells us about our Creator and His purpose for the world. But it also gives us the most accurate understanding of mankinds perplexing nature, and why we behave the way we do.

Harvard Professor Robert Coles has interviewed hundreds of people in many different societies. When asked what he had learned from his research on human nature, Dr. Coles pointed to the Bible on his desk and said, "Nothing I have discovered about the makeup of human beings contradicts, in any way, what I learn from the Hebrew prophets. . . . and from Jesus and the lives of those he touched."

The writings of others and our own experience can teach us much about why we behave as we do. But only the Bible tells us that our sinful heart is the heart of our problem, and that we can be changed from within by trusting Jesus.

Yes, the Bible is still relevant. Are you growing in your love for this ancient book?

Vernon Grounds

Your heart and conscience cannot guide,
For they're deceived by sin inside;
But if you want to see what's true,
The Word of God will mirror you.

Hess

The Bible is a mirror that let's us see ourselves as God
sees us.

Read Psalms 19:7–11 (see "Mirror Analogy")

From Our Daily Bread, copyright 2003 by Radio Bible Class
(RBC) Ministries, Grand Rapids Michigan. Reprinted by
permission. (From Our Daily Bread segment of Thursday
September 25, 2003) All rights reserved.

Introduction

All of the "religions" in the world have one thing in common; they're all trying to promote peace, love, and harmony in the world, and subdue hatred and violence. Secularism tries to do the same thing (as opposed to secular hatred and violence.) Some musically inclined secularists come up with songs expressing, all they want to do is celebrate another day of living, and they have to fight for their right to party ("Let's eat, drink, and be merry, for tomorrow, we die", 1 Corinthians 15:32.)

Christianity, on the other hand, is not just a religion. It is a relationship with the only living God; not just an extension of philosophies handed down by a prophet.

People who desire to follow the Creator of the universe are promised to inherit ever-lasting life with God. But those who lack faith and choose to not believe in the spiritual God, who spent 33 years enveloped in a physical body on the earth, which He created, and where He voluntarily paid the penalty for our sins, are destined to exist forever in a state of anguish, longing, thirst, and hunger of which only the Creator and voluntary Atoner of our sins can remedy, as described in the various metaphorical parables of Hell. (Revelation 1:5.)

But, in order to learn about the way to eternal life is to read the Holy Bible.

Many people say they don't read the Bible because "it's too hard to understand", "it contradicts itself", "it doesn't make any sense." But the Bible isn't made to make sense, it's made to make faith.

"We walk by faith, not by sight," (2 Corinthians 5:7.) "Faith comes by hearing, and hearing by the word of God," (Romans 10:17.) " 'My thoughts are not your thoughts, nor are your ways my ways,' says the Lord." (Isaiah 55:8.)

But another reason why people don't like to read the Bible is because, like a mirror, it shows them their sinful self and points them to Judgement Day. But "God is a merciful God," (Deuteronomy 4:31.) And He does not take pleasure in the death of the wicked. . . ." (Ezekiel 33:11,) "but that all should come to repentance"; (2 Peter 3:9.)

Younger people either have no role models, inadequate role models, personal problems, or are just immaturely rebellious causing them to be involved in drug and alcohol abuse, bullying, and gang violence. They have lost their path in this maze of life, and need (and want?) to find meaning for their life

In the worldly realm, there are book clubs which like to read fictitious novels, and discuss the plot, and speculate what is dwelling in the characters minds. But how often do we get involved in studying God's word? We don't like it when people ignore us, and God doesn't like to be ignored either, (Exodus 20:3–6.) One way we ignore God is by substituting worldly books for the Bible.

This Bible Study guide is intended to help you find what God says about Himself, about you, about life, and the way to escape Hell before Judgement Day arrives.

Inside you will find scriptures that define, make main points about, and/or exemplify the listed topics. But you may also find scriptures that seem to contradict other scriptures. This is where we get into Bible Study, (1 Corinthians 2:13.)

(I personally recommend "Key Word" Bible Studies, by the late Dr. Duane Spencer; Seminaryathome.com.)

You will also find certain scriptures repeated, (cross references,) since some scriptures cover more than one topic. Specific topics in Psalms 119 will be listed separately. But the entire 119th Psalm is an expression of the Greatest Commandment. Also, the scriptures are listed in the order they appear in the Bible, for easier finding. Imperative and definitive scripture references are marked with an asterisk (*).

This Bible Guide is also intended to help you develop the interest and habit of reading Gods word. (Romans 12::2) Incidentally, on a segment of the John Tesh radio program, Mr. Tesh said the most shop-lifted book (at least in the United States) is the Bible. This is a vivid picture of the hunger for Gods word. (Proverbs 28:11)

But, look out! God says that there eventually be a famine through out the world—a hunger of hearing Gods word, and will not be found. (Amos 8:11–13; John 6:66–68)

This Bible Guide is intended to help you find Jehovah's

answer to life, and to help you find and know God personally, as He already knows you personally. (Jeremiah 1:5) And for the unsaved, help you find the way to salvation.

Read this guide slowly and carefully. And read it over, because things you may not understand the first time you may come to your understanding a second or third time, or later. (This is how this guide was composed.)

Every day we are surrounded by good as well as evil distractions that make us take God for granted. Being in a solitary place, away from distractions, is the best place to go and ponder and mediate on Gods word, and to pray (talk) to God.

Start reading the Holy Bible. Find God (Jehovah); find yourself; and find what no (other) religion can show you—the way to eternal life.

You can know God to the limit of what He has revealed about himself, his commandments, and guidelines by reading His word the Holy Bible.

There may be some questions you have that the Bible has no answer for. But everything we need to know is in God's word. The overall commandment and guideline to perusing a relationship with God is found in the greatest commandment.

This Bible Study guide is in no way perfect. Since there are a number of various modern translations of the Bible, there can still be a little confusion, at times. Two examples are the words "temptation" and "blessed."

For computer users, I highly recommend logging on to Seminaryathome.com, for Bible Studies with the late Doctor Duane Spencer.

Neither Dr. Spencer nor Word of Grace are affiliated with this book.

A lot of "religious" books merely tell us how to live our lives in peace and harmony. But the Holy Bible, whose Author is the living Creator of the universe, tells us about the way provided to escape the eternal condemnation of God—His own beloved Son, whom was begotten by the Holy Ghost to the Virgin Mary.

No other man-appointed "god" accomplished the horrible task of suffering the wrath of God for our sins.

"You will seek Me and find me, when you search for Me with all your heart."

Jeremiah 29:13

"Come to Me all of you who labor and are heavy laden, and I will give you rest. Take My yoke upon you and learn from Me, for I am meek and lowly in heart, and you will find rest for your souls. For My yoke is easy, and My burden is light."

Matthew 11:28–30

All we like sheep have gone astray;
We have turned, everyone to our own way.
God sent His Son, the Savior,
To save His people He favors;
God and sinners to reconcile,
Whose sins continue to pile.
God is ready to forgive,
Sinners granted to forever live.
Jesus died for our loss;
Crucified on a cross.
This is the reason for the first Christmas Day,
To find Jesus, the Life, the Truth, and the Way.

THIS IS

WHAT LIFE

IS ALL ABOUT

Contents

xiv

Special Features

Abortion

Genesis 2:7	Psalms 102:18
Genesis 16:9–10	Psalms 139:13–16
Genesis 17:5–8	Proverbs 6:16–17
Genesis 19:30–38	Isaiah 43:7
Genesis 21:13	Isaiah 44:1–2
Genesis 24:60	Isaiah 49:1*
Genesis 25:20–23	Jeremiah 1:1–9
Exodus 1:(21)	Ezekiel 18:4
Exodus 20:13	Amos 1:13
Exodus 21:22–23	Zechariah 12:1
Leviticus 17:11–14*	Matthew 1:18–25
Deuteronomy 30:19*	Matthew 19:13–15
Psalms 24:1	Luke 1:1–64
Psalms 51:5	Acts 7:19
Psalms 71:6	Romans 8:29–30
Psalms 78:1–8	Romans 9:11–16

(Also, see Age of Accountability," "Children")

(*Also, see "Prophesies of Christ," Christmas Event)

Actions Speak Louder Than Words

2 Timothy 2:15	1 John 3:16–18
James 2:5–26	

Addictions/Obsessions

Exodus 20:1–6	1 Corinthians 10:31
Deuteronomy 6:4–5	Revelation 2:1–4
Psalms 119	

Adultery/Fornication

Genesis 38	Proverbs 5:3–6
Exodus 20:14	Proverbs 5:18–20
Leviticus 18	Proverbs 6:20–29
Leviticus 19:20	Proverbs 6:32
Deuteronomy 5:18	Proverbs 7
2 Samuel 11	Proverbs 30:20

Ezekiel 16 (:15–17)*

Ezekiel 23:13–16*

Hosea Ch. 1–Ch. 2

Matthew 5:27–30

Matthew 14:1–4

Mark 10:11–12

Romans 6:12–13

Romans 12:1–2

1 Corinthians 5:1–13

1 Corinthians 6:9–10

1 Thessalonians 4:1–8

Hebrews 13:4

Jude 1:(5–7)

(Also, see "Idolatry," "Pornography." The key words for "Pornography" are, Images, Lust, and "Harlotry.")

Age of Accountability

Genesis 2:8–3:24

Numbers 14:26–35A (31)

Deuteronomy 1:39

2 Samuel 12:1–23

Matthew 18:14

Acts 7:19

Romans 9:6–26 (11)

(Numbers quotes God speaking; Deuteronomy is Moses elaborating what God declared.)

Angels

Psalms 104:1–4

Psalms 148:1–6

Hebrews 1:13–14

2 Peter 2:4

Anger/Wrath

Nehemiah 9:17

Psalms 4:4–5

Psalms 37:8

Psalms 103:8–9

Psalms 145:8

Proverbs 14:17A

Proverbs 14:29

Proverbs 15:1

Proverbs 15:18

Proverbs 16:24

Proverbs 16:32

Proverbs 19:11

Proverbs 19:19

Proverbs 22:24–25

Proverbs 29:11

Proverbs 29:22

Proverbs 30:33

Ecclesiastes 7:9

Ecclesiastes 10:4

Nahum 1:3

Matthew 5:21–24

Matthew 21:12–13

Mark 11:15–17

Luke 12:49

Luke 19:45–46

John 2:13–16

Ephesians 4:26–27

James 4:1

Anti-christs

Matthew 24:4–5
Matthew 24:11
Mark 13:5–6
Mark 13:21–23

2 Thessalonians 2:1–12
1 John 2:18–26
1 John 4:1–3
2 John 1:7

(Also, see "False Christs")

Anxiety

Psalms 23
Psalms 46:10
Proverbs 12:25
Isaiah 40
Matthew 6:19–34

Matthew 11:28–30
Philippians 4:6–7
Philippians 4:19
James 5:7–8

Apostasy/Falling Away

2 Corinthians 6:14–18
2 Thessalonians 2:1–12

1 Timothy 4:1–5
Revelation 18:(4)

(Also, see "Bad Company," "Repentance")

Bad Company

Proverbs 12:26
Proverbs 22:24–25
1 Corinthians 5:9–13
1 Corinthians 15:32–33
2 Corinthians 6:14–18

2 Thessalonians 3:6–7
2 Thessalonians 3:14–15
Revelation 18:(4)
Revelation 21:8
Revelation 22:14–15

Baptism

Matthew 3
Matthew 20:22–23
Matthew 28:18–20
Mark 1:4
Mark 16:15–16
Luke 3:1–22 (16*)
Luke 12:50
Luke 23:39–43
John 1:19–33

John 3:22–23
John 4:1–2
Acts 1:4–5
Acts 2:38–41
Acts 8:9–38
Acts 10:34–38
Acts 11:16*
Acts 13:23–24
Acts 16:14–15

Acts 18:8
Acts 19:1–5
Romans 6:1–4
1 Corinthians 12:12–13

Galatians 3:26–29
Ephesians 4:1–6
Colossians 2:11–12
1 Peter 3:21

Beatitudes

Psalms 1
Psalms 32:1–2
Psalms 37:9–11
Proverbs 10:30

Matthew 5:1–12
Luke 6:20–26
Romans 4:7–8

Bible Study

Romans 12:2
1 Corinthians 2:13

1 Timothy 4:16

Blindness

Isaiah 6:9–10
Isaiah 42:1–7
Matthew 5:8
Matthew 13:13–15
Matthew 15:14
Luke 4:18
John 9

John 12:37–40
Romans 11:1–10
2 Corinthians 4:1–4
Ephesians 4:17–24 (18)
2 Peter 1:1–11 (9)
1 John 2:9–11

Blood

Genesis 4:1–10
Numbers 35:9–34 (19–25)
Leviticus 17:1–14*
Psalms 40:6
Matthew 26:27–28
Matthew 27:1–4
Mark 14:23–24
Luke 22:20
Acts 20:17–28
Romans 5:9
Ephesians 1:3–7
Ephesians 2:13

Colossians 1:12–14
Colossians 1:19–20
Hebrews 9:11–14
Hebrews 9:19–22
Hebrews 10:4–10
Hebrews 10:19–22
1 Peter 1:18–19
1 John 1:7
Revelation 1:4–5
Revelation 5:1–9
Revelation 7:9–14
Revelation 19:11–13

Born Again

John 1:12–13

John 3:1–8

John 6:63

Romans 10:8–10

Titus 3:1–7

1 Peter 1:22–23

(Also, see "Salvation")

Brevity of Life

Psalms 39:4–6

Psalms 89:47–48

Psalms 90:4–12

Psalms 102:24–28

Psalms 119:84

Psalms 144:4

James 4:14B

Bullying

Psalms 129

Psalms 142

Psalms 143

Proverbs 1:10–19

Matthew 5:21–22

Matthew 7:12

Matthew 7:15–20

Matthew 22:37–39

1 Corinthians 3:16–17

1 John 3:14

(Also, see "Fruits of the Holy Spirit," "Gang Violence,"
"Second Greatest Commandment," "Golden Rule," "Murder,"
"Oppression," "Pride.")

Children

Psalms 127:3–4

Matthew 18:1–14

Matthew 19:13–15

Mark 9:36–37

Mark 10:13–16

Luke 9:46–48

Luke 18:15–17

(Also, see "Abortion," "Age of Accountability")

A Christmas Carol
(Ebenezer Scrooge)

Luke 16:19–31

Romans 10:17

Christmas

*Isaiah 49:1
(Matthew 1:1–17)
(Luke 3:23–28)
Luke 1:1–80

Matthew 1:18–25
Luke 2:1–40
Matthew 2:1–23
Luke 2:41–52

(*Also, see "Abortion," "Prophesies About Christ")

Christmas Trees

Jeremiah 10:1–5
(Psalms 115:1–8)

Psalms 135:15–18

Christmas Tree Lighting Ceremonies

Exodus 32

Daniel 3

(Also, see "Idolatry")

Circumcision

Genesis 17:10–27
Genesis 21:1–4
Genesis 34:1–19
Exodus 12:43–51
Leviticus 12:1–3
Joshua 5:1–12
Jeremiah 4:4
Luke 2:21
Acts 7:8
Acts 15:1–29
Acts 16:1–5
Romans 2:25–29

Romans 3
Romans 4:1–13
Romans 15:8
1 Corinthians 7:17–19
Galatians 2:1–10
Galatians 5:1–6
Galatians 6:11–15
Philippians 3:1–6
Colossians 2:11
Colossians 3:1–11
Colossians 4:7–11
Titus 1:10–11

Communion/Last Supper

Matthew 26:26–30
Mark 14:22–26

Luke 22:14–20
1 Corinthians 11:23–26

(Also, see "Passover")

Complaining

Exodus 17:1–7
Numbers 11
Psalms 142:1–2
1 Corinthians 10:8–10
Ephesians 5:20

Philippians 2:12–15
2 Timothy 2:23–26
James 5:9
1 Peter 4:9

Contentment

Exodus 16:18
Psalms 23
Psalms 37
Psalms 46:10
Proverbs 30:7–9*
Ecclesiastes 6:1–2
Luke 3:14
Luke 22:35

2 Corinthians 3:4–6
2 Corinthians 8:15
2 Corinthians 12:7–10
Philippians 4:10–13
Philippians 4:19
1 Timothy 6:3–11
Hebrews 4:14–16
Hebrews 13:5–6

(Also, see "Coveting")

Coveting

Exodus 20:17
Deuteronomy 5:21
2 Samuel 11:1–12:23

Psalms 119:37
Colossians 3:5

Creation

Genesis 1:1–2:7
Genesis 2:19
Genesis 5:1–2
Genesis 6:7
Nehemiah 9:5–6
Job 26:13
Job 32:8
Job 33:4
Psalms 8:3
Psalms 19:1
Psalms 24:1–2
Psalms 29:7–11
Psalms 33:6–9

Psalms 74:15–17
Psalms 89:8–12
Psalms 94:9–10
Psalms 95:1–6
Psalms 100:3A
Psalms 102:25–27
Psalms 104
Psalms 107:23–25
Psalms 115:15
Psalms 119:90
Psalms 136:5–9
Psalms 148:1–6
Proverbs 3:19–20

Proverbs 20:12
Ecclesiastes 12:7
Isaiah 40:25–26
Isaiah 42:5
Isaiah 43:7
Isaiah 43:15
Isaiah 44:2A
Isaiah 44:24
Isaiah 45:7–18
Isaiah 48:1–3
Isaiah 48:12–13
Isaiah 51:15
Jeremiah 10:10–13
Jeremiah 31:35
Jeremiah 51:15

Amos 9:6
Zechariah 12:1
John 1:1–4
Romans 1:18–20
1 Corinthians 11:8–12
1 Corinthians 12:14–26
Ephesians 3:9
Colossians 1:15–18
Hebrews 1:1–2
Hebrews 1:8–12
Hebrews 3:4
Hebrews 11:3
Revelation 3:14
Revelation 4:9–11

Crime

Ecclesiastes 8:11
Jeremiah 11

Romans 13:1–4

The Cross (The Crucifixion)

Deuteronomy 21:22–23
Matthew 10:38
Matthew 16:24–25
Matthew 27:27–54
Mark 8:34–35
Mark 10:17–22
Mark 15:21–39
Luke 9:23–24
Luke 14:25–27
Luke 23:26–47
John 19:15–37
Acts 5:30–32
Acts 10:39–43

Acts 13:28–32
1 Corinthians 1:17–18
Galatians 3:13
Galatians 5:11
Galatians 6:11–15
Ephesians 2:13–16
Philippians 2:5–8
Philippians 3:17–21
Colossians 1:19–20
Colossians 2:11–14
Hebrews 12:1–2
1 Peter 2:21–24

(Also, see "Blood," "Sin")

Cross Dressing

Deuteronomy 22:5

Cussing/Profanity

Exodus 20:7
Psalms 34:13
Proverbs 8:13
Proverbs 15:4
Proverbs 15:23
Proverbs 16:24

Matthew 12:36–37
Ephesians 4:29–32
Colossians 3:5–11
Colossians 4:6
James 1:21
James 3:1–12

Dancing

Exodus 15:20
Exodus 32:(19)
Judges 11:34
1 Samuel 18:6
2 Samuel 6:11–15 (14)

Psalms 30:10–12
Psalms 149:(3)
Psalms 150:(4)
Ecclesiastes 3:1–4
Jeremiah 31:1–14 (4, 13)

Death Penalty

Genesis 2:16–17
Genesis 3
Genesis 9:6
Numbers 15:32–36
Numbers 35:30–31
John 5:24
John 8:51
Acts 2:22–24
Romans 5:10–14
Romans 6:1–10
Romans 6:15–23

Romans 7:5–25
Romans 8:1–6
1 Corinthians 15:20–56
2 Corinthians 1:9–10
2 Timothy 1:8–10
Hebrews 2:9
James 5:19–20
1 John 3:14
Revelation 1:18
Revelation 20:11–15

Debts

Deuteronomy 15:1–11
Deuteronomy 23:19
Proverbs 17:18

Proverbs 22:7
Proverbs 22:26–27
Isaiah 55:1–2

Delayed Entry Program

Deuteronomy 24:5

Depression

Psalms 23	Matthew 5:12
Psalms 34	Matthew 11:28–30
Psalms 148	John 11:1–6
Psalms 149	John 14:1–3
Psalms 150	Revelation 21:1–4

Divorce/Annulment (and Remarriage)

Deuteronomy 24:1–4	Matthew 19:1–10
Isaiah 44:21–22	Mark 10:1–12
Jeremiah 3:1–4:4	Luke 16:18
Malachi 2:13–16	Romans 7:1–3
Matthew 5:31–32	1 Corinthians 7:10–16

Dog Food

Matthew 7:6	Mark 7:24–30
Matthew 15:21–28	

Don't Be Partnered with Unbelievers

Deuteronomy 7:1–6	1 Corinthians 10:14–22
Judges Ch. 13–Ch. 16	1 Corinthians 15:33
Ezra 9	2 Corinthians 6:14–18
Proverbs 12:26	Revelation 18:1–8
1 Corinthians 5:9–13	

Double Minded (Spiritually/Carnally)

Romans 8:1–11	James 1:5–8

Doubting

Matthew 8:23–27	Mark 9:24
Matthew 9:18–26 (24)	John 20:24–29
Matthew 11:1–6	James 1:5–6

Drunkenness/Intoxication

Proverbs 20:1
Proverbs 23:20–21
Proverbs 23:29–35
Proverbs 31:4–7
Matthew 15:7–20
Romans 13:13–14

1 Corinthians 5:9–13
Galatians 5:19–21
Ephesians 5:1–10
1 Timothy 5:23
1 Peter 4:1–5

Empathy

Exodus 3:9
Exodus 22:21
Exodus 23:9
Leviticus 25:17
Proverbs 21:13

John 11:28–36 (35)
Romans 12:15
1 Corinthians 12:12–27
Galatians 6:2

Employees/Employers

Deuteronomy 24:14–15
Matthew 20:1–16
Luke 17:7–10
Ephesians 6:5–9
Philippians 2:14

Colossians 3:22
1 Timothy 6:1–5
Titus 2:9–10
1 Peter 2:18–23

Encouraging Others

Proverbs 12:25
Proverbs 15:23
Proverbs 16:24
Galatians 6:1–2

Ephesians 4:29–32
1 Peter 1:22
1 Peter 3:8–9
1 Peter 4:8–9

Everything Made New

Isaiah 42:9
Isaiah 65:17–19
2 Corinthians 5:17

Ephesians 4:17–24
Revelation 21

Evolution

Genesis 1:24–28	1 Corinthians 1:25A
Genesis 2:7	1 Corinthians 3:19–20
Genesis 5:1–2	1 Corinthians 15:39
(Psalms 2)	1 Corinthians 15:45–49
Psalms 29:9	2 Corinthians 5:7
Psalms 100:3	2 Timothy 4:1–5
Luke 3:23–28	2 Peter 2:1–9
Romans 1:22–25	

(Also, see "Creation")

Fair Weather Friends

Psalms 41:9	Jeremiah 9:4–6

Faith
(Failing Always, I Trust Him)

Genesis 15:1–6	Luke 5:1–10
Joshua 21:43–45	Luke 17:5–6
2 Kings 1	John 16:33
Psalms 31:24	Romans 1:16–17
Psalms 34	Romans 3:27–28
Psalms 42:5–11	Romans 5:1–2
Psalms 131	Romans 8:23–25
Proverbs 3:5–6	Romans 8:31–39
Isaiah 40:28–31	Romans 10:17
Daniel (Book)	Romans 14:23
Habakkuk 2:4	1 Corinthians 2:1–5
Matthew 8:23–27	1 Corinthians 15:12–19
Matthew 11:28–30	1 Corinthians 15:57
Matthew 14:25–33	2 Corinthians 4:18
Matthew 15:21–28	2 Corinthians 5:7
Matthew 21:18–22	Galatians 3:19–25
Mark 4:35–41	Philippians 3:3
Mark 7:24–30	Philippians 4:13
Mark 9:14–29 (24)	Philippians 4:19

Hebrews 10:38
Hebrews 11:(1)
Hebrews 12:1–2
James 1:5–6

James 2:14–26
1 Peter 5:6–7
1 John 5:4

False Christs/Prophets/Witnesses

Deuteronomy 4:2
Deuteronomy 13:1–5
Proverbs 12:22
Proverbs 14:12
Proverbs 16:25
Proverbs 19:9
Proverbs 24:21–22
Isaiah 30:8–11
Jeremiah 5:30–31
Jeremiah 14:11–16
Jeremiah 23:16–40
Jeremiah 27:8–16
Jeremiah 29:8–9
Jeremiah 29:21–23
Ezekiel 13
Matthew 16:1–12
Matthew 23:13–39
Matthew 24:3–5
Matthew 24:11
Matthew 24:24
Mark 13:21–22
Luke 12:1–3

Luke 17:20–24
Romans 11:8–10
Romans 16:17–18
2 Corinthians 11:10–15
Galatians 1:6–12
Colossians 2:8–10
1 Thessalonians 5:21
2 Thessalonians 2:1–12
1 Timothy 1:3–4
2 Timothy 2:14–18
2 Timothy 3:13
2 Timothy 4:1–5
Titus 1:10–11
2 Peter 2
2 Peter 3:14–18
1 John 2:22–26
1 John 4:1–3
2 John 1:7–11
Jude 1:4–7
Revelation 6:1–2
Revelation 22:18–19

(Also, see "Antichrists")

Family Values

Genesis 1:26–28
Genesis 2:24–25
Genesis 38:1–2
Exodus 20:12
Exodus 20:14

Exodus 21:17
Leviticus 19:3
(Leviticus 19:32)
Leviticus 20:9
Deuteronomy 6:1–9*

Deuteronomy 8:5

Deuteronomy 11:18–21*

Deuteronomy 27:16

Deuteronomy 31:9–13

Joshua 24:14–15

Psalms 78:1–8

Psalms 127:1

Psalms 127:3

Psalms 128

Psalms 133

Proverbs 6:20–22

Proverbs 13:1

Proverbs 13:24

Proverbs 14:1

Proverbs 15:5

Proverbs 15:17

Proverbs 15:20

Proverbs 17:1

Proverbs 17:6

Proverbs 17:14

Proverbs 17:21

Proverbs 17:25

Proverbs 19:13

Proverbs 19:18

Proverbs 19:26

Proverbs 20:7

Proverbs 20:11

Proverbs 20:20

Proverbs 20:29–30

Proverbs 22:6

Proverbs 22:15

Proverbs 23:13–14

Proverbs 23:22

Proverbs 23:24–25

Proverbs 24:3–4

Proverbs 28:24

Proverbs 29:15

Proverbs 30:11

Proverbs 30:17

Proverbs 31:10–31

Matthew 15:4–9

Mark 7:10–13

2 Corinthians 12:14

Colossians 3:18–21

1 Thessalonians 2:11–12

1 Timothy 5:1–8

Titus 2:1–8

Hebrews 3:4

1 Peter 5:5

3 John 1:4

Fasting

Exodus 34:27–28

Deuteronomy 8:1–3

Judges 20:26

1 Samuel 7:6

1 Samuel 31:13

2 Samuel 1:12

2 Samuel 12:15–23

1 Kings 21:27

1 Chronicles 10:12

Ezra 8:21–23

Ezra 9:5

Nehemiah 1:4

Nehemiah 9:1

Esther 4:3

Esther 9:31

Psalms 35:13

Psalms 63:1–5

Psalms 69:10

Psalms 109:24

Isaiah 58

Jeremiah 36:6

Daniel 6:18

Daniel 9:3
Joel 2:12–14
Zechariah 7:1–7
Matthew 4:1–4
Matthew 6:16–18
Matthew 9:14–15
Matthew 17:14–21
Mark 2:18–20

Luke 4:1–4
Luke 5:33–35
Luke 18:9–14
Acts 10:30
Acts 13:1–3
Acts 14:23
1 Corinthians 7:1–5

Fear

Psalms 23:4
Psalms 25:12–15
Psalms 34:4
Psalms 56:11
Psalms 111:10
Psalms 112
Psalms 118:6
Proverbs 1:7
Proverbs 3:7
Proverbs 8:13
Proverbs 9:10

Proverbs 14:27
Proverbs 19:23
Proverbs 22:4
Ecclesiastes 12:13–14
Matthew 10:28
Luke 12:4–7
2 Timothy 1:7
Hebrews 10:30–31
Hebrews 13:6
1 John 4:18

Fellowship

Psalms 133
Romans 12:15
Galatians 6:2

Hebrews 10:24–25
James 5:16

First Fruits

Genesis 4:3–5
Exodus 13:1–2
Exodus 13:11–16
Leviticus 23:9–10
Numbers 3:12–13
Numbers 3:40–45
Numbers 8:16–17
Deuteronomy 15:19A

Deuteronomy 26:1–15
2 Chronicles 31:1–8 (5)
Nehemiah 10:35–37
Proverbs 3:9
Romans 8:23
Romans 11:16
James 1:18

Foods

Genesis 9:1–3
Exodus 16:1–31
Leviticus 11
Deuteronomy 8:1–3
Deuteronomy 12:15
Deuteronomy 12:20
Deuteronomy 14:1–21
Deuteronomy 15:19–23
Psalms 78:1–31
Proverbs 15:17
Matthew 4:4

Matthew 15:10–20
Matthew 22:1–4
Mark 1:6
Luke 15:23
John 4:30–34
Acts 10:9–16
Romans 14:1–3
1 Corinthians 8:8
1 Corinthians 10:25–31
1 Timothy 4:1–5
Hebrews 13:9

Foolishness

Proverbs 12:15–16
Proverbs 14:1
Proverbs 14:9
Proverbs 15:5
Proverbs 17:12

Proverbs 18:2
Proverbs 26:11
1 Corinthians 1
1 Corinthians 2:14–16
1 Corinthians 3:18–20

Forgiveness

Exodus 32:30–32
Leviticus 19:18
2 Chronicles 6:36–40
Psalms 98:6–8
Psalms 130:1–4
Proverbs 10:12
Proverbs 24:17–18
Matthew 6:14–15
Matthew 18:21–35
Mark 11:25–26

Luke 6:36–37
Luke 7:36–50
Luke 11:4
Luke 17:3–4
Luke 23:33–34
2 Corinthians 2:3–11
Ephesians 4:31–32
Colossians 3:12–13
2 Timothy 4:16

Fruits of the Holy Spirit

Ezekiel 18:1–9
Matthew 21:18–19
Mark 11:12–14
Mark 11:20–21

Luke 3:7–14
Luke 10:25–37
Luke 13:6–9
John 15:1–8

John 15:16–17
Romans 8:9
Romans 12:9–21
Galatians 5:22–26
Ephesians 4:11–13

Ephesians 5:8–14
Colossians 3:12–17
Titus 1:15–16
James 2:14–26
1 John 3:17–18

Gang Violence/Organized Crime

Exodus 23:2A
Proverbs 1:10–19

Jeremiah 7:11

(Also, see "Second Greatest Commandment", "Crime",
"Golden Rule", "Bad Company")

(In descriptions of God, Jesus, and the Holy Spirit, you may also
find revelations of the Trinity, or Tri-unity. Also, see Trinity.)

God Hears Prayers of the Righteous

1 Kings 9:1–3
Psalms 6:9
Psalms 18:1–6
Psalms 28:6
Psalms 34:14–16
Psalms 66:18–20

Proverbs 15:8
Proverbs 15:29
Isaiah 59:1–4
John 9:31
1 Peter 3:12

God is the Bibles' Author

Psalms 119:105
Psalms 119:160
Proverbs 21:30
Proverbs 30:5–6
Isaiah 40:13–14
Jeremiah 36
Matthew 1:18–25 (22)
Matthew 2:12–15 (15)
Matthew 10:19–20
Luke 1:68–71 (70)
Luke 3:1–6 (4)

Acts 3:19–24 (21)
Romans 1:1–2
1 Corinthians 2:4–10
Galatians 1:11–12
1 Thessalonians 2:13
2 Timothy 3:16–17
Hebrews 1:1–2
Hebrews 4:12
2 Peter 1:20–21
Revelation 22:18–19

God is Calling

Exodus 3
1 Samuel 3:1–10
Jeremiah 1:1–9
Matthew 4:18–22

Matthew 20:16
Luke 19:1–10
Acts 9:1–9

God is a Consuming Fire

Genesis 19:1–29
Exodus 24:12–18
Deuteronomy 4:24
Deuteronomy 9:3
1 Kings 18:1–40
Psalms 21:8–9
Psalms 50:1–3
Psalms 89:46

Psalms 97:1–3
Isaiah 30:27
Daniel 3
Zephaniah 1:18
Hebrews 12:29
Revelation 8
Revelation 20:11–15

God is the Creator—See Creation

God is Eternal (No Beginning; No End)

Job 36:26
Psalms 90:1–4
Psalms 93:1–2
Psalms 102:24–28
Psalms 106:48
Isaiah 40:8
Isaiah 63:16
Jeremiah 10:10

Micah 5:2
John 1:1–2
John 5:26
John 17:5
Acts 15:18
Colossians 1:17
Hebrews 6:2–7:24
Hebrews 9:14

God is First and Last

Isaiah 43:10–11
Isaiah 44:6–8
Isaiah 48:12–13
Mark 12:28–34 (32)
1 Corinthians 8:6
Ephesians 4:1–6

Revelation 1:8
Revelation 1:11A
Revelation 1:17–18
Revelation 2:8
Revelation 22:13

God is the Great 'I Am'
(Jesus is the Great 'I Am'; Jesus is God)
(Also, see "Trinity")

Genesis 28:10–16
Exodus 3:1–15
Deuteronomy 32:39
Isaiah 43:10–13
Matthew 18:20
Matthew 24:5
John 8:12
John 8:58
John 10:7

John 10:14
John 13:19
John 14:6
John 14:11
Hebrews 11:6
Revelation 1:8
Revelation 1:11A
Revelation 1:18
Revelation 22:20

God is Jealous

Exodus 20:5
Exodus 34:14
Deuteronomy 4:24

Deuteronomy 6:13–15
Nahum 1:2
Zephaniah 1:14–18

God is King of Kings and Lord of Lords

Deuteronomy 10:17
Revelation 17:14

Revelation 19:16

God is Light

Exodus 13:21
Exodus 33:12–34:35
Psalms 27:1
Psalms 119:105
Isaiah 9:2
Isaiah 60:1–3
John 1:1–13
John 3:19–21

John 8:12
John 9:5
John 12:35–36
John 12:46
2 Corinthians 4:6
Colossians 1:9–18
Revelation 21:23

God is Omnipotent (All Powerful)

Genesis 1:1	Matthew 14:13–36
Genesis 2:7	Matthew 15:32–39
Genesis 7:23	Matthew 20:29–34
Genesis 19:12–29	Matthew 21:18–19
Exodus 3	Matthew 28:1–10
Job 34:21–28	Mark 6:30–56
Psalms 8:3–4	Mark 7:31–37
Psalms 19:1	Mark 8:1–9
Psalms 29	Mark 8:22–25
Psalms 33	Mark 9:14–29
Psalms 94:8–11	Mark 11:12–14
Psalms 95:1–5	Mark 16:1–8
Psalms 96:1–5	Luke 8:22–25
Psalms 100:3	Luke 8:40–56
Psalms 102:25	Luke 24:1–12
Psalms 104	John 2:1–9
Psalms 107:35	John 6:1–21
Psalms 135:6	John 10:17–21
Matthew 8:23–27	John 11:17–44

God is Omnipresent (Everywhere)

Genesis 28:10–16	Psalms 139:7–12
1 Kings 8:27	Proverbs 15:3
Psalms 33:13–14	

God is Omniscient (All Knowing)

Job 35:10–11	John 6:22–26
Psalms 94:8–11	John 16:30
Psalms 147:5	1 Corinthians 2:10
Proverbs 15:3	1 John 3:20
Mark 9:33–37	

God is the Only Living God
(Jehovah, Jesus, Yahweh)

Deuteronomy 4:35–39

Deuteronomy 32:39

1 Kings 18:1–40

2 Kings 19:19

Psalms 86:10

Isaiah 6:1–5

Isaiah 43:10–11

Isaiah 44:6–8

Isaiah 45:5–7

Isaiah 45:20–22

Isaiah 46:9–10

Jeremiah 10:10

John 1:1

John 1:18

John 12:37–41

John 13:19–20

John 20:28

1 Corinthians 8:6

Ephesians 4:4–6

1 Thessalonians 1:2–9

Titus 2:13

Hebrews 1:8

Hebrews 10:31

God is a Potter

Genesis 2:7

Job 10:9

Job 33:6

Psalms 2:9

Psalms 31:12

Isaiah 29:16

Isaiah 30:8–14

Isaiah 41:25

Isaiah 45:9

Isaiah 64:8*

Jeremiah 18:1–6*

Jeremiah 19:1–11

Lamentations 4:2

Romans 9:1–26

Revelation 2:27

God is a Refuge

Psalms 9:9–10

Psalms 27:10

Psalms 46

Psalms 57:1

Psalms 61

Psalms 62:7

Psalms 91:1–2

Psalms 141:8

Psalms 142:5

Psalms 144:1–2

Matthew 11:28–30

God is the Rock (Jesus)

1 Samuel 2:1–2	Psalms 71:1–3
2 Samuel 22:(1–4)	Psalms 78:34–35
2 Samuel 22:(47)	Psalms 89:24–26
2 Samuel 23:1–3	Psalms 92:15
Psalms 18:(1–2)	Psalms 94:22
Psalms 18:(31)	Psalms 95:(1)
Psalms 18:(46)	Isaiah 28:16
Psalms 27:4–5	Matthew 7:24–27
Psalms 28:1–2	Matthew 16:18
Psalms 31:1–5	Luke 6:47–49
Psalms 42:5–11	Romans 9:33
Psalms 61	1 Peter 2:1–8
Psalms 62:1–7	

(Also, see "God is a Refuge", "Spiritual Water", that comes
from the Rock

God is the Savior
(Jesus is the Savior; Jesus is God)

2 Samuel 22:3	Ephesians 5:23
2 Kings 13:5	Philippians 3:20
Psalms 106:21	1 Timothy 1:1
Isaiah 19:20	1 Timothy 2:1–6
Isaiah 43:1–11	1 Timothy 4:10
Isaiah 45:15–21	2 Timothy 1:8–10
Isaiah 49:26	Titus 1:3–4
Isaiah 60:16	Titus 2:10–13
Isaiah 63:8	Titus 3:4–6
Jeremiah 14:7–9	2 Peter 1:1–11
Hosea 13:4	2 Peter 2:20
Luke 1:46–47	2 Peter 3:2
Luke 2:11	2 Peter 3:18
John 4:42	1 John 4:14–16
Acts 5:30–31	Jude 1:25
Acts 13:23	

God is Sovereign (over-all Ruler)

Psalms 50

Psalms 97

Psalms 113

Psalms 115

Isaiah 45:5–7

Matthew 28:18

Revelation 22:12–13

God is Unchanging

Malachi 3:6

Hebrews 13:8

** God Knows Your Heart and Mind
(Attitudes, Emotions, Intentions, Motives, Thoughts)

Genesis 6:1–8 (5)

Genesis 16:(11D, 13)

1 Samuel 2:3

1 Samuel 16:7

1 Kings 8:38–40

1 Chronicles 28:9

1 Chronicles 29:17

2 Chronicles 6:29–30

Psalms 7:8–10

Psalms 15

Psalms 32:1–2

Psalms 34:18

Psalms 37:4–5

Psalms 37:29–31

Psalms 40:8

Psalms 44:20–21

Psalms 51:17

Psalms 62:4

Psalms 94:11

Psalms 95:7–11

Psalms 125:4

Psalms 139:1–10

Psalms 139:23–24

Proverbs 4:4

Proverbs 6:12–15

Proverbs 11:20

Proverbs 12:2

Proverbs 15:8

Proverbs 16:2

Proverbs 17:3

Proverbs 19:21

Proverbs 20:27

Proverbs 21:2

Proverbs 24:12

Proverbs 27:19

Isaiah 29:13–15

Isaiah 66:2

Jeremiah 17:5

Jeremiah 17:9–10

Jeremiah 29:11–13

Zechariah 8:17

Matthew 1:18–20

Matthew 9:3–4

Matthew 12:34–35

Matthew 15:1–20

Matthew 22:37–38

Matthew 23:1–28

Mark 2:6–8

Mark 7:1–23

Luke 6:6–8

Luke 6:45

Luke 9:46–48

Luke 11:37–54

Luke 12:34

Luke 16:15
John 2:23–25
John 6:64
Romans 2:14–16
Romans 8:27
Romans 10:10
1 Corinthians 4:5

1 Thessalonians 2:4
Hebrews 3:8–10
Hebrews 4:11–13
1 Peter 5:5
1 John 3:16–23
Revelation 2:23

God's Benefits

Psalms 37:4
Psalms 103

Psalms 116:12–19
Psalms 145:8–9

God's Elect (Chosen People; Predestination)

Psalms 33:12
Psalms 65:4
Psalms 105:6
Isaiah 41:8–9
Matthew 1:21
Matthew 10:1–7
Matthew 15:24
Matthew 18:11–13
Matthew 20:16
Matthew 22:1–14
Luke 4:24–30
Luke 19:1–10
John 1:12–13
John 6:29
John 6:37–45
John 6:65
John 6:70
John 10:24–30
John 11:49–52
John 15:16–19
Acts 2:46–47
Acts 9:15–16
Acts 13:48
Romans 8:30–39

Romans 9:6–29
Romans 11:1–10
Romans 11:26–29
1 Corinthians 1:9
2 Corinthians 13:5–6
Galatians 4:21–31
Ephesians 1:3–12
Philippians 1:29
Colossians 3:11–13
1 Thessalonians 1:1–4
1 Thessalonians 5:9–10
2 Thessalonians 2:13–14
2 Timothy 1:8–9
2 Timothy 2:10
2 Timothy 2:19
Titus 1:1–2
1 Peter 1:1–2
1 Peter 2:9–10
2 Peter 1:1–11
1 John 4:1–6
1 John 4:14–15
1 John 5:13
2 John 1:1
Revelation 17:14

(Also, see Question #6)

God's Name in Vain

Exodus 20:7
Leviticus 22:32–33
Deuteronomy 5:11
Psalms 8:1
Psalms 34:1–3
Psalms 139:19–20
Proverbs 30:9
Matthew 6:9
Matthew 12:36–37

Luke 11:2
Acts 2:38
Acts 3:16
Acts 4:12
Acts 22:16
Philippians 2:9–10
2 Timothy 2:19
1 John 3:23
1 John 5:13

(Also, see "Cussing")

God's Promise to Abraham and Sarah

Genesis 15:18–21
Genesis 17:15–22
Genesis 18:1–15
Genesis 21

Psalms 105:42
Romans 9:9
Hebrews 6:9–20

God's Promise to David

1 Samuel 13:14
1 Samuel 16:1–13
2 Samuel 7:1–17
1 Kings 1
2 Chronicles 21:7
Jeremiah 33:19–26
Zechariah 9:9
Matthew 9:27

Matthew 12:22–23
Matthew 21:1–11
Mark 10:46–48
Luke 2:1–4
John 7:40–44
Acts 13:22–23
Revelation 22:16

God's Promise of Eternal Life

John 3:16
John 5:24
Titus 1:1–2
Hebrews 4:1–3

Hebrews 9:11–15
James 1:12
1 John 2:25

God's Promise of the Holy Spirit

Luke 24:49

John 14:16

John 14:26

John 16:7

Acts 2:33

The Promised Land

Exodus 3:1–8

Deuteronomy 28:9

Deuteronomy 29:10–13

Deuteronomy 31:7

Deuteronomy 34:1–4

1 Kings 8:56

Acts 7:17

2 Peter 3:13

Revelation 21:1–4

God's Promise of a Savior

Genesis 22:7–8

Isaiah 53:7

Luke 2:8–11

John 1:29

John 1:36

John 3:26–30

Acts 13:22–39

(Also, see "Prophesies About Christ")

God's Will (Plan)

Psalms 40:6–8

Jeremiah 31:33

Matthew 6:10

Matthew 12:46–50

Mark 3:31–35

Luke 8:19–21

Luke 22:42

Luke 23:33–34

John 4:31–34

John 5:30

John 6:38–40

Acts 14:1–22

Romans 8:28

Ephesians 1:1–11

Ephesians 5:17

Philippians 2:12–13

Colossians 1:9

1 Thessalonians 5:16–22

Hebrews 10:9–10

1 Peter 3:17

1 John 2:17

"Golden Rule"

Proverbs 21:13

Proverbs 25:21–22

Matthew 7:12*

Luke 6:27–36 (31)*

Luke 10:25–37

Romans 12:14–15

(Also, see "Fruits of the Holy Spirit,"
"Second Greatest Commandment.")

Government

Genesis 9:6
Genesis 11:1–9*
Exodus 18:13–27
(Exodus 22:18)
Exodus 22:28
Numbers 35:30–31
Deuteronomy 16:18–20
Deuteronomy 17:8–20
2 Samuel 23:2–4
2 Chronicles 7:14**
Psalms 2
Psalms 118:9
Proverbs 14:34
Proverbs 16:12
Proverbs 28:9

Matthew 18:18
Matthew 22:15–21
Matthew 23
Mark 3:24
Mark 12:38–40
Luke 20:21–25
Luke 20:46–47
John 19:10–11
Acts 5:29
Acts 23:5
Romans 13:1–7
1 Timothy 2:1–2
Titus 3:1
Hebrews 13:17
1 Peter 2:13–16

(* One World Government)
(** Also, see "Repentance")

Grace Vs. Works
(God's Riches at Christ's Expense)

Genesis 15:1–6
Genesis 22:1–8
Proverbs 14:12
Proverbs 16:25
Isaiah 4:1
Matthew 7:21–23
Luke 18:9–14
John 5:1–15
John 6:28–29
John 9:1–34
Acts 8:26–39
Romans 2:13–16
Romans 3:1–5:2
Romans 4
Romans 9:30–33

Romans 10:1–13
Romans 11:1–7
Galatians 2:11–21
Galatians 3
Galatians 5:1–6
Ephesians 2:8–10
Ephesians 4:7
Philippians 1:6
Philippians 2:12–14
2 Timothy 1:8–10
Titus 3:4–5
Hebrews 4:16
James 2:14–26(*)
1 Peter 1:13–16

(* Also, see "Fruits of the Holy Spirit")
(Also, see "Faith")

Great Commission

Isaiah 52:7

Matthew 28:18–20

Mark 16:15

Luke 24:44–47

Romans 10:14–15

(Also, see "Witness")

** Greatest Commandment

Exodus 20:1–3

Exodus 33:18

Deuteronomy 4:29–31

Deuteronomy 5:6–7

Deuteronomy 6:(5)*

Deuteronomy 10:12

Deuteronomy 11:13–21

Deuteronomy 13:1–5

Deuteronomy 26:16–19

Deuteronomy 28

Deuteronomy 30

Joshua 24:14–15

1 Kings 2:1–4

1 Chronicles 28:9

2 Chronicles 15:1–2

2 Chronicles 31:2–8

Ezra 7:10

Ezra 8:22

Psalms 1:1–3

Psalms 19:7–11

Psalms 27:4–10

Psalms 34:8–10

Psalms 37:1–5

Psalms 40:1–8

Psalms 63:6–8

Psalms 69:29–33

Psalms 81:8–16

Psalms 97:10–12

Psalms 103:17–18

Psalms 111:10

Psalms 112:1–3

Psalms 115

Psalms 119

Psalms 128:4

Psalms 147:10–11

Proverbs 3:1–9

Proverbs 8:13

Proverbs 15:9

Proverbs 18:10

Proverbs 23:17–18

Proverbs 28:5

Ecclesiastes 12:13–14

Daniel 1:8

Hosea 13:4–16

Micah 6:8

Matthew 4:8–10

Matthew 6:33

Matthew 10:37–39

Matthew 22:34–38*

Mark 8:34

Mark 10:17–22

Mark 12:28–34

Luke 4:8

Luke 9:23

Luke 10:25–27

Luke 12:4–5

Luke 12:31

Luke 14:26–33

John 5:23

John 8:31

John 8:51

John 14:15–24

John 15:9–13
Romans 6:15–23
1 Corinthians 7:19
1 Corinthians 10:31
Colossians 3:1–3
Colossians 3:15–17

Hebrews 11:6
1 John 2:3–5
1 John 3:20–23
1 John 5:1–5
2 John 1:6
Revelation 22:14

(Also, see "Separation of Church and State")

(Second) Greatest Commandment

Leviticus 19:34*
Psalms 35:19
Psalms 41:1–3
Psalms 133
Proverbs 15:1
Proverbs 25:21–22
Zechariah 7:8–10
Matthew 22:34–39*
Mark 12:28–31*
Luke 6:27–42
Luke 10:25–37

Acts 20:35
Romans 12:14–15
Romans 12:19–21
Romans 13:8–10
1 Corinthians 10:32–33
Galatians 5:13–14
Philippians 2:3–4
1 Peter 2:17
1 John 3:18
1 John 4:20–21

(Also, see "Fruits of the Holy Spirit", "Golden Rule")

Greatest Love of All

John 15:13   1 John 3:16

Hair (Head Coverings)

1 Corinthians 11:1–16

Here-after (Life After Death)

Proverbs 23:17–18

Hell (Death)

Genesis 2:15–17
Genesis 3:1–19
Psalms 116:3–4
John 5:24

John 8:51
1 Corinthians 15:54–56
Revelation 20:11–15

Hell (Fire)

Isaiah 66:24
Daniel 3
Matthew 5:22
Matthew 18:8–9
Mark 9:43–48

2 Thessalonians 1:3–10
James 3:6
Jude 1:5–7
Revelation 20:7–15

Hell (Hell)

Psalms 9:17
Psalms 55:15
Proverbs 7:6–27
Proverbs 23:13–14

Proverbs 27:20
Isaiah 14:9
Matthew 23:33
Luke 12:4–5

Hell (Outer Darkness)

Psalms 107:10–12
Psalms 139:12
Isaiah 9:2
Matthew 8:12
Luke 22:53

1 Peter 2:9
2 Peter 2:17
Jude 1:5–7
Jude 1:12–13

Hell (The Pit, Bottomless)

Job 33:22
Psalms 28:1
Psalms 49:(9)
Psalms 143:7
Isaiah 38:18

Ezekiel 31:16
Jonah 2:6
Zechariah 9:11
Revelation 20:1–3

Hell (Second Death)

Revelation 2:10–11
Revelation 20:6

Revelation 20:11–15
Revelation 21:8

Hell (Sheol)

Job 11:8
Job 26:6
Psalms 16:10

Psalms 116:3–4
Isaiah 38:18

Holidays

Colossians 2:16–17

Holy Spirit (Holy Ghost)

Genesis 1:1–2	Acts 5:1–11
Genesis 6:3	Acts 8:29
Exodus 23:20–23	Acts 10:44–45
Judges 14:1–6	Acts 13:1–4
Isaiah 11:1–2	Acts 16:6
Matthew 3:11–17	Acts 20:22–23
Matthew 4:1	Acts 20:28
Matthew 10:19–20	Romans 8:2
Matthew 12:32	Romans 8:9
Mark 1:10–13	Romans 8:14
Mark 3:28–30	Romans 8:26–27
Luke 1:35	Romans 15:13
Luke 3:21–22	1 Corinthians 2:10–11
Luke 12:11–12	1 Corinthians 6:19
Luke 24:39	1 Corinthians 12:1–11
John 1:32	2 Corinthians 3:17
John 3:1–8	Galatians 4:6
John 4:22–26	Galatians 5:22–23
John 6:63	Ephesians 2:19–22
John 7:37–39	Ephesians 4:25–32
John 14:6–26	Ephesians 5:18
(16–17) (26)	Hebrews 3:7–11
John 15:26–27	1 Peter 1:1–2
John 16:1–15	1 Peter 4:14
Acts 2:4	

Homosexuality

Genesis 1:27–28A	Romans 1:21–32
Genesis 2:22–24	1 Corinthians 6:9–10
Genesis 5:1–2	1 Corinthians 11:8–12
Genesis 19:1–29	2 Peter 2:4–11 (6–8)
Leviticus 18:22*	Jude 1:5–7
Leviticus 20:13*	

(Also, see "Requirements for Church Elders")

Hope

Psalms 31:23–24	Psalms 130:(7)
Psalms 33:16–22	Psalms 147:10–11
Psalms 42:(5–11)	Romans 8:(24–25)
Psalms 43:(5)	

Humility

1 Kings Ch. 21–Ch. 29	Proverbs 29:23
Ezra Ch. 9–Ch. 10	Matthew 11:28–30
Psalms 18:27	Mark 10:13–16
Psalms 39:4–7	Luke 10:19–20
Psalms 138:6	Luke 14:7–14
Psalms 147:6	Luke 18:9–17
Proverbs 22:4	John 13:1–15
Proverbs 25:6–7	1 Peter 5:5–6
Proverbs 27:2	

Hypocrisy (Hypocrite = Actor)

Proverbs 11:9	Matthew 23:13–33
Proverbs 25:26	John 8:1–11
Isaiah 52:5	Romans 2:17–24
Ezekiel 36:22	Titus 1:15–16

Idolatry

Exodus 20:3–6	1 Kings 14:1–11
Exodus 20:22–23	1 Kings 16:21–26
Exodus 25:17–22	2 Kings 17
Exodus 32	2 Kings 19:17–19
Leviticus 19:4	2 Chronicles 33:1–17
Leviticus 26:1–2	Psalms 81:9
Deuteronomy 4:15–40	Psalms 82
Deuteronomy 12:1–4	Psalms 89:6–12
Deuteronomy 12:29–32	Psalms 96:4–6
Deuteronomy 17:1–5	Psalms 97:7
Deuteronomy 27:15	Psalms 115:1–8
Joshua 23:6–8	Psalms 119:36–37
Joshua 23:14–16	Isaiah 42:8

Isaiah 44
Isaiah 45:15–20
Jeremiah 10:1–16
Jeremiah 25:1–7 (6)
Jeremiah 51:17–19
Ezekiel 14:1–11
*Ezekiel 16:15–17
Ezekiel 23:13–16
Daniel 3

Hosea 13:4
Micah 5:10–14
Habakkuk 2:18–20
Romans 1:18–32
1 Corinthians 6:9–10
Galatians 4:8–9
Colossians 3:5–6
Revelation 2:1–7 (4)

(*Also, see "Adultery," "Pornography")

Immaculate Conception
(Pope Pius IX; Dec. 8, 1854)
(Virgin Mary Born Without a Sin Nature?)

Psalms 14:1–3
Matthew 9:13
Mark 2:17
Luke 1:46–48

Luke 5:31–32
Romans 3:11–12
Romans 3:23
Revelation 22:18–19

Incest

Leviticus 18:1–17

Intermarriages

Genesis 34
Judges 2:11–3:6
Ezra Ch. 9–Ch. 10
Nehemiah 13:23–31

Romans 10:12–13
2 Corinthians 6:14
Galatians 3:28

Jealousy

Genesis 4:3–8
Exodus 20:4–5
Exodus 34:14

Proverbs 6:32–35
1 Corinthians 10:14–22 (22)
1 Corinthians 13:4

Jesus Came to Save

Isaiah 61:1–3
Matthew 1:18–21
Matthew 18:11
Luke 4:16–21

Luke 9:51–56
John 3:16–18
John 6:38–40
John 12:47

Jesus is First in Authority

Isaiah 9:6   John 5:26–27
Matthew 28:18

Jesus is "First-born"

Exodus 4:18–23   1 Corinthians 15:20–23
Psalms 89:20–27   Colossians 1:12–20
Acts 26:22–23   Hebrews 1:1–14
Romans 8:29   Revelation 1:4–5

(See "Question", #12)

Jesus is a Friend

John 15:13–15

Jesus is the "Lamb" of God

Genesis 22:1–8   Acts 8:32–33
Exodus 12:1–30   1 Peter 1:18–21
Leviticus 3:7   Revelation 5:11–13
Isaiah 53:1–7   Revelation 6:1
Ezekiel 46:12–15   Revelation 19:1–9
John 1:29–36

Jesus is Our (Only) Mediator (Priest)

John 14:6   Hebrews 4:14–5:10
Acts 4:8–12   Hebrews 7:11–28
Romans 8:34   Hebrews 8
Ephesians 2:14–18   Hebrews 9
Ephesians 3:8–12   Hebrews 12:22–24
1 Timothy 2:5–6   1 John 2:1–2

Jesus is Our Redeemer (Savior)

Job 19:25   Psalms 44:23–26
Psalms 19:14   Psalms 49:5–8
Psalms 25:22   Psalms 49:15*
Psalms 26:8–11   Psalms 69:16–18
Psalms 34:19–22   Psalms 103:1–5 (4)

Psalms 107:2

Psalms 111:9

Psalms 130:7–8

Isaiah 35:8–10

Isaiah 43:1–7 (1)

Isaiah 44:21–23

Isaiah 49:25–26

Isaiah 50:1–2

Isaiah 51:11

Isaiah 52:1–3

Isaiah 59:20

Isaiah 60:15–16

Isaiah 62:11–12

Isaiah 63:16

Hosea 13:14

Luke 2:36–38

Luke 21:28

Romans 3:24

Romans 8:23

1 Corinthians 1:30

Galatians 3:13

Ephesians 1:1–14 (7)*

Ephesians 4:30

Colossians 1:12–14*

1 Timothy 2:5–6*

Hebrews 9:11–15

1 Peter 1:18–21*

Revelation 5:9

Revelation 14:1–4

(Also, see "Blood", "Jesus is the Lamb of God")

Jesus is the Son of God (the Father)

Psalms 2:(7–9)

Isaiah 7:14–16

Isaiah 9:6–7

Daniel 3:25

Hosea 11:1

Matthew 3:13–17

Matthew 7:21

Matthew 8:28–29

Matthew 10:32–33

Matthew 11:27

Matthew 12:50

Matthew 14:25–33

Matthew 16:13–17

Matthew 17:1–5

Matthew 26:39

Matthew 26:57–64

Matthew 27:40–43

Matthew 28:19

Mark 3:7–12

Mark 5:1–7

Luke 1:35

Luke 4:40–41

Luke 8:28

Luke 9:35

Luke 10:22

Luke 22:66–71

Luke 23:34

John 1:29–34*

John 1:49

John 3:16–18

John 5:17–23

John 6:65–69

John 8:16–29

John 8:36

John 10:15A

John 10:30–38

John 14:6–24

John 15:1

John 17

John 20:21

John 20:31

Acts 8:37

Acts 9:20
Romans 1:1–16
Romans 8:1–5
1 Corinthians 15:47
2 Corinthians 11:31
Galatians 4:4–7
Hebrews 1:5
1 John 1:1–3
1 John 1:21–26

1 John 2:20–26
1 John 3:8
1 John 3:20–23
1 John 4:14–15
1 John 5
2 John 1:1–3
2 John 1:7–11
Jude 1:4
Revelation 3:21

Jesus Prayed

Matthew 11:25–26
Matthew 26:39–44
Mark 14:35–36
Luke 5:16

Luke 6:12
Luke 10:21
John 11:41–42
John 17

(Also, see "Prayer")

Jesus Prayed For Future Believers

John 17:20–26

Jesus is the "Vine"

John 15:1–8

Romans 11:(16–21)

Jesus is the Word of God

John 1:1–5
John 1:14

1 John 5:6–8
Revelation 19:11–13

Judgement (Day)

Psalms 9:1–8
Psalms 11:6
Psalms 68:2–3
Psalms 75
Psalms 76:7–9
Psalms 90:8
Psalms 96:13
Psalms 98:9

Psalms 119:120
Psalms 119:126
Psalms 119:155
Psalms 122:1–5
Proverbs 10:25
Proverbs 11:4
Ecclesiastes 8:11
Isaiah Ch. 2–Ch. 3

Isaiah 13
Isaiah 17:7–11
Isaiah 66:15–18
Jeremiah 17:1–13
Ezekiel 33:11
Daniel 7
Daniel 12
Joel 2:1
Amos 4:11–13
Micah 5:5–15
Zephaniah 1
Zephaniah 2:4–15
Malachi 3:5–7
Matthew 8:11–12
Luke 12:42–48
Luke 13:1–5
Luke 16:19–31
John 3:18
John 5:22–30
John 8:15–16

John 12:46–50
Acts 10:42
Acts 17:30–31
Romans 2:1–16
1 Corinthians 11:31–32
1 Corinthians 15:26
2 Corinthians 5:10
2 Thessalonians 1:6–10
2 Timothy 4:1–2
Hebrews 4:13
Hebrews 10:30–31
1 Peter 4:17
1 Peter 5:4
2 Peter 3:3–7
Jude 1:12–16
Revelation 20:4
Revelation 20:11–15
Revelation 21:6–8
Revelation 22:14–15

Judgement Day Comes Unexpected

Isaiah 2
Joel 2:1
Matthew 24:36–51
Matthew 25:1–13
Mark 13:32–37
Luke 21:20–36
Acts 1:7

1 Thessalonians 5:1–4 (2)
2 Thessalonians 2:3
1 Timothy 6:13–15
1 Peter 4:7
2 Peter 3:10*
Revelation 3:1–6 (3)
Revelation 16:15

Judging

Ezekiel 33:7–11
Matthew 7:1–5
Matthew 7:15–20
Luke 6:37
Luke 9:51–56
John 8:1–16
Romans 2:1–3

Romans 14:1–13
1 Corinthians 5:1–13
1 Corinthians 8
Ephesians 5:11–14
James 4:11–12
James 5:19–20

(Also, see "Witness")

Judging By Appearance

Leviticus 19:15

1 Samuel 16:7

John 7:24

2 Corinthians 10:7

The Last Shall Be First, and the First, Last

Genesis 27

Genesis 38:24–30

Genesis 48:1–19

Matthew 19:30

Matthew 20:16

Matthew 21:28–32

Mark 9:35

Mark 10:31

Luke 13:30

Law Suits

Deuteronomy 25:1–3

1 Corinthians 6:1–8

Laziness

Genesis 2:1–2

Genesis 2:15

Proverbs 6:6–11

Proverbs 10:4–5

Proverbs 10:26

Proverbs 19:24

Proverbs 20:4

Proverbs 20:13

Proverbs 22:13

Proverbs 24:30–34

Proverbs 25:19

Proverbs 26:13–16

Proverbs 30:24–28

Proverbs 31:10–31

Jeremiah 40:10

Matthew 9:37

Matthew 25:14–30

Ephesians 2:8–10

Ephesians 4:1

Colossians 3:23–24

2 Thessalonians 3:6–15

James 1:25

1 Peter 4:10–11

Liberty (Freedom)

John 8:30–36

2 Corinthians 3:17

Galatians 5:1

Galatians 5:13–15

James 1:25

1 Peter 2:13–17

Loneliness

1 Kings 8:57–58
Psalms 9:10
Psalms 22:1–2
Psalms 23
Psalms 28:6–7
Psalms 34:4–10
Psalms 40:1–3
Psalms 51:17
Psalms 63:1–5
Psalms 100
Psalms 107:8–9
Psalms 146–150
Zechariah 13:7
Matthew 8:20
Matthew 26:31
Matthew 26:47–56
Matthew 27:46
Matthew 28:20B
Luke 12:6–7
Luke 22:47–65
John 16:32

Lottery

Proverbs 16:33
Proverbs 18:18
Luke 1:5–9
Acts 1:15–26

(Also, see "Wealth")

Love (Charity)

Psalms 97:10
Proverbs 10:12
Proverbs 27:5
Matthew 5:43–48
John 3:16
John 15:9–13
Romans 8:35–39
Romans 12:9–21
Romans 13:8–10*
1 Corinthians 13*
Galatians 5:22–23
Ephesians 4:1–3
Colossians 3:12–14
1 Thessalonians 5:14
1 Timothy 1:5
1 John 3:16–18
1 John 4:7–11
1 John 16–21
1 John 5:3
2 John 1:6

Love Song

Song of Solomon (Song of Songs)

Lying

Exodus 20:16
Exodus 23:1–2B
Leviticus 19:11
Deuteronomy 5:20
Psalms 31:18
Psalms 52
Psalms 58:3–5
Psalms 119:163
Psalms 120:2
Proverbs 6:16–19
Proverbs 12:19
Proverbs 12:22
Proverbs 13:5

Proverbs 19:5
Proverbs 19:9
Proverbs 19:22
Proverbs 21:6
Proverbs 21:28
Proverbs 25:18
Proverbs 26:28
Jeremiah 7:1–7
Ephesians 4:25
Colossians 3:9–10
2 Thessalonians 2:1–12
Titus 1:1–2
Hebrews 6:18

Marriage

Genesis 1:26–28
Genesis 2:18–25
Genesis 12:10–20
Genesis 38:1–2
Leviticus 18:22
Leviticus 20:13
Esther 1
Proverbs 5:18–20
Proverbs 12:14
Proverbs 18:22
Proverbs 19:14
Proverbs 20:25
Proverbs 21:9
Proverbs 21:19
Proverbs 25:24
Proverbs 27:15–16
Proverbs 30:21–23A
Proverbs 31:10–31
Ecclesiastes 9:9
Song of Solomon
Isaiah 62:1–5
Jeremiah 3:(14)
Jeremiah 31:31–32

Malachi 2:13–16
Matthew 19:3–10
Matthew 25:1–13
Mark 2:18–22
Mark 10:1–12
Mark 12:19–25
Luke 5:33–39*
Luke 20:27–36
Romans 7:1–3
1 Corinthians 7:1–16
1 Corinthians 7:38–40
1 Corinthians 11:3
2 Corinthians 6:14–18
Ephesians 5:22–23
Colossians 3:18–19
Hebrews 13:4
1 Peter 3:1–7
Revelation 2:17
Revelation 3:12
Revelation 19:7–9
Revelation 21:1–2
Revelation 21:9
(* = Compatibility)

Men and Women

Deuteronomy 22:5
Proverbs 11:22

1 Corinthians 14:34–36
1 Timothy 2:8–15

Mercy

Nehemiah 9:17
Psalms 18:25
Psalms 103:8–18
Psalms 118:1–4
Psalms 136
Psalms 145:8
Proverbs 11:17
Proverbs 14:21
Proverbs 14:31
Proverbs 21:13
Proverbs 22:22–23
Proverbs 25:21–22
Proverbs 28:13
Proverbs 28:27

Proverbs 29:7
Lamentations 3:22
Matthew 5:7
Luke 6:27–36
Luke 10:30–37
Colossians 3:12–13
1 Timothy 1:12–16
Hebrews 4:14–16
James 2:13
James 3:17
James 5:11
1 Peter 1:3
1 Peter 2:9–10
Jude 1:21

Mirror Analogy

Proverbs 27:19

James 1:22–25

Murder

Genesis 4:1–15
Genesis 9:6
Exodus 20:13
Exodus 21:22–25
Leviticus 19:16–17
Leviticus 24:17
Leviticus 24:21
Numbers 35:9–34
  (19–25 Blood)

Deuteronomy 5:17
Deuteronomy 19:11–13
Deuteronomy 27:25
2 Samuel 11
2 Samuel 12:1–23
Proverbs 6:16–19
Matthew 5:21–22A
Acts 7:17–19
1 John 3:14–15

Musical Instruments

2 Samuel 6:5
1 Kings 1:40
1 Chronicles 13:7–8
1 Chronicles 15:16
1 Chronicles 15:28
1 Chronicles 16:42
2 Chronicles 5:11–14
Ezra 3:10–13
Nehemiah 12:27

Psalms 57:7–8
Psalms 68:25
Psalms 92:1–4
Psalms 98:4–9
Psalms 144:9
Psalms 149:3
Psalms 150
Habakkuk 3:19

Mustard Seed Parables

Matthew 13:31–32
Matthew 17:20
Mark 4:30–32

Luke 13:18–19
Luke 17:5–6

My Way

Proverbs 12:5
Proverbs 14:12
Proverbs 16:2
Proverbs 16:9
Proverbs 16:25

Proverbs 19:2
Proverbs 20:24
Proverbs 21:2
Isaiah 53:6
1 Peter 2:25

Mystery

Psalms 25:14
Luke 10:23–24
Romans 8:25
Romans 16:25–27
1 Corinthians 2:6–10
Ephesians 3

Ephesians 5:30–33
Colossians 1:24–27
Colossians 2:1–10
2 Thessalonians 2:7
1 Timothy 3:14–16
Revelation 10:7

Nakedness

Genesis 2:25
*Genesis 3
Nehemiah 4:1–5
Job 29:14

Psalms 32:1–2
Psalms 85:1–2
Proverbs 10:12
Proverbs 17:9

Isaiah 47:1–3

Romans 4:7–8

*Isaiah 61:10

Hebrews 4:13

Micah 1:11

*Revelation 3:14–18

Matthew 10:24–26

Revelation 16:15

Luke 12:1–2

Sin is shame, illustrated by nakedness. God covers our sin with salvation.

New Covenant

Isaiah 59:20–21

Hebrews 8:7–13

Jeremiah 31:31–34

Hebrews 9:11–15

Romans 11:26–27

Hebrews 10:11–18

1 Corinthians 11:23–25

Hebrews 12:24

Oaths

Matthew 5:33–37

James 5:12

Oppression

Exodus 1:1–22

Psalms 103:6

Exodus 3:1–8

Psalms 106:42–43

Leviticus 25:17

Psalms 119:121–122

Judges 10

Psalms 123

Psalms 3

Psalms 140:6–8

Psalms 9

Psalms 146:5–7

Psalms 10

Proverbs 3:31–32

Psalms 12:5

Ecclesiastes 5:8

Psalms 13

Isaiah 49:26

Psalms 17:(9)

Isaiah 51:12–13

Psalms 25:18

Isaiah 61:1–3

Psalms 42:9–11

Jeremiah 7:6–7

Psalms 44:23–26

Jeremiah 50:31–34

Psalms 54:1–3

Zechariah 7:10–14

Psalms 55:(3)

Matthew 5:11–12

Psalms 56:(1)

Luke 4:16–21

Psalms 62:10

Acts 10:34–39

Psalms 72:14

2 Corinthians 4:8–10

Psalms 76:8–9

James 5:13

Parables of Heaven

Isaiah 11:6–10
Isaiah 35
Matthew 13:24–50
Matthew 18:21–35
Matthew 20:1–16
Matthew 22:1–14
Matthew 25:1–30

Mark 4:30–32
Luke 13:18–21
Luke 14:15–24
Romans 14:17
Revelation 19:7–9
Revelation 21:2–3
Revelation 21:9–27

Parables of Sheep

Numbers 27:15–17
2 Samuel 24:17
1 Kings 22:17
1 Chronicles 21:17
2 Chronicles 18:16
Psalms 44:11
Psalms 44:22
Psalms 49:13–15
Psalms 74:1
Psalms 78:52
Psalms 79:13
Psalms 95:7
Psalms 100:1–3
Psalms 119:176
Isaiah 53:1–7
Jeremiah 12:1–3
Jeremiah 50:6
Jeremiah 50:17

Ezekiel 34
Zechariah 13:7
Matthew 9:35–36
Matthew 10:5–6
Matthew 10:16
Matthew 15:24
Matthew 18:10–14
Matthew 25:31–33
Mark 6:34
Mark 14:27
Luke 15:1–7
John 10:1–30
John 21:15–17
Acts 8:32
Romans 8:36
Hebrews 13:20
1 Peter 2:25

Parables of Wheat and Weeds (Tares)

Matthew 13:24–30
Luke 3:16–17
*Acts 8:1–3

*Acts 9:1–31
*Acts Ch. 21–Ch. 28
*1 Timothy 1:12–16

(* Saul/Paul, Wheat among weeds; Gods elect.)

Partiality (Prejudice)

Leviticus 19:14–15
Leviticus 19:35–36
Proverbs 18:5
Proverbs 22:2
Proverbs 24:23
Proverbs 28:21
John 7:24

Acts 10:34–35
Romans 2:7–11
Romans 10:12–13
Galatians 3:28
Colossians 3:25
James 2:1–9

(Also, see "Judging By Appearance", Racism)

Passover (Feast of Unleavened Bread)

Exodus 12
Exodus 13:1–10

Deuteronomy 16:1–6
Romans 3:21–26 (25)

Peace

Psalms 23
Psalms 85:7–10
Psalms 119:165
Ecclesiastes 3:8
Isaiah 9:6
Isaiah 48:22
Nahum 1:15
Zechariah 9:9–10
Matthew 10:12–13
Matthew 10:34–37
Mark 9:50
Luke 2:14
Luke 12:51–53

John 14:27
John 16:33
John 20:19
Romans 5:1–2
Romans 8:6
1 Corinthians 14:33
2 Corinthians 5:17–21
Ephesians 2:14–18
Philippians 4:6–7
Colossians 1:19–20
1 Thessalonians 5:2–3
2 Thessalonians 3:16
Hebrews 7:1–2

Peer Pressure

Genesis 3
Proverbs 1:10–19
Romans 12:2

1 Corinthians 15:32–33
2 Timothy 2:22
James 4:7–8

(Also, see "Bad Company", "Bullying", "Gang Violence",
"Read the Bible", "Sin", Temptation," "Worldliness.")

Pets
(Owned, and Other Farm Animals)

Exodus 20:17　　　　　　　Psalms 8:4–8
Deuteronomy 22:1–7　　　　Proverbs 12:10

Pope
(God On Earth?, Holy Father?)

Matthew 1:23　　　　　　　John 17:11
Matthew 23:9

Pornography

Exodus 20:1–6　　　　　　Matthew 5:27–30
Exodus 20:14　　　　　　　Matthew 18:6
*Ezekiel 16:15–17　　　　　Mark 9:42
*Ezekiel 23:13–16　　　　　Luke 17:2
Psalms 101:3

(Also, see "Adultery," "Idolatry." Key words, "Images," "Lust,"
"Harlotry.")

Possibilities/Impossibilities

Matthew 17:14–21　　　　　Mark 14:32–36
Matthew 19:23–26　　　　　Luke 1:37
Matthew 24:24　　　　　　 Luke 18:24–27
Matthew 26:39　　　　　　 Acts 2:22–24
Mark 9:23　　　　　　　　 Hebrews 6:17–18
Mark 10:23–27　　　　　　 Hebrews 10:4
Mark 13:22　　　　　　　　Hebrews 11:6

Practice What You Learn

Deuteronomy 8:1　　　　　 James 2:14–26
James 1:22–25

Practice What You Preach

Romans 2:21–24　　　　　　1 Corinthians 9:13–14

(Also, see "Hypocrisy", "Judging")

Praise

Deuteronomy 10:20–21
Judges 5:3
2 Samuel 22:4
1 Chronicles 16:7–36
Nehemiah 9
Psalms 22:22–26
Psalms 33:1–3
Psalms 34:1–3
Psalms 40:16
Psalms 44:8
Psalms 50:23
Psalms 65:1
Psalms 66
Psalms 67
Psalms 71:6
Psalms 72:15
Psalms 84:4–5
Psalms 89:1–18
Psalms 113
Psalms 119:164
Psalms 145
Psalms 147:1

Psalms 148
Psalms 149
Psalms 150
Proverbs 31:10–31
Song of Solomon/
   Song of Songs
Jeremiah 33:9
Daniel 4:34–35
Matthew 21:14–17
Luke 2:13–14
Luke 24:52–53
John 12:42–43
Romans 2:29
Philippians 4:8
Hebrews 2:12
Hebrews 13:15–16
1 Peter 2:9
1 Peter 2:13–14
Revelation 4:11
Revelation 5:11–12
Revelation 15:3–4
Revelation 19:5–6

Prayer

Exodus 3
Deuteronomy 4:7
Deuteronomy 8:10
2 Chronicles 7:13–14
Nehemiah 1:4–11
Psalms 109
Psalms 145:18–19
Jeremiah 29:11–13
Jeremiah 33:1–3
Daniel 6
Daniel 9:20–23

Matthew 6:5–13
Matthew 14:22–23
Matthew 26:36–44
Mark 6:45–46
Mark 14:35–39
Luke 5:16
Luke 6:12
Luke 10:1–2
Luke 10:21–22
Luke 11:1–4
Luke 18:1–8

48

Luke 22:31–32
Luke 22:41–46
Luke 23:42–43
John 11:41–43

John 17
Romans 8:26–27
James 4:1–10
James 5:16–18

Pride

Psalms 10:2–3
Psalms 75
Psalms 119:21
Psalms 138:6
Proverbs 3:5
Proverbs 6:16–19
Proverbs 8:13
Proverbs 11:2
Proverbs 13:10
Proverbs 14:3
Proverbs 16:5
Proverbs 16:18
Proverbs 21:24
Proverbs 22:10
Proverbs 24:17–18
Proverbs 25:6–7
Proverbs 27:2
Proverbs 28:25
Proverbs 29:23
Proverbs 30:32
Ecclesiastes 7:8B
Isaiah 14:12–20
Jeremiah 50:31–32
Ezekiel 28:1–19

Daniel 4
Daniel 5
Obadiah 1:(1–4)
Matthew 23:1–12
Luke 10:17–20
Luke 14:7–11
Luke 18:9–14
Romans 12:3
Romans 12:16
1 Corinthians 4:6–7
1 Corinthians 8:12
1 Corinthians 10:12
2 Corinthians 10:12–18
2 Corinthians 11:30
2 Corinthians 12:1–7
2 Corinthians 12:11
Galatians 5:25–26
Galatians 6:3
Galatians 6:14
1 Timothy 6:3–5
James 4:10
James 4:13–17
1 Peter 5:5–6
1 John 2:16–17

Prison/Discipline/Detention

Psalms 118:18
Psalms 119:71
Proverbs 3:11–12
Proverbs 13:18
Proverbs 15:10
Matthew 11:1–6

Luke 7:18–23
Acts 12:1–11
Acts 21:26–28:31
Romans 13:1–4
Hebrews 12:3–11

(Also, see "Tough Times")

Proof God Exists

Psalms 19:1

Psalms 107:23–43

Romans 1:18–20

Hebrews 11:3

Prophesies About Christ

Genesis 22:1–8 (8)

Exodus 12:46C

Numbers 24:15–19

Deuteronomy 18:15–19

Deuteronomy 32:43

Psalms 22

Psalms 65:1–3

Psalms 69

Psalms 89

Psalms 110

Psalms 118:22–23; 26

Isaiah 2

Isaiah 7:10–16

Isaiah 9

Isaiah 10:17

Isaiah 11:1–5

Isaiah 11:10

Isaiah 16:1–5

Isaiah 19:20

Isaiah 42:1–9

*Isaiah 49: (1)

Isaiah 50

Isaiah 52:13–15

Isaiah 53

Isaiah 59:20–21

Isaiah 61:1–3

Jeremiah 23:5–6

Jeremiah 31:15

Jeremiah 32:6–9

Jeremiah 33:15–18

Daniel 7:13–14

Hosea 11:1

Micah 5:2–5

Nahum 1:15

Zephaniah 1:7

Zechariah 3:8

Zechariah 6:9–15

Zechariah 9:9–10

Zechariah 12:10

Zechariah 13:7

Matthew 1:23

Matthew 2:1–6

Matthew 2:16–18

Matthew 4:12–16

Matthew 12:18–20

Matthew 15:21–28 (24)

Matthew 26:31

Matthew 26:47–56

Matthew 27:9

Matthew 27:32–35

Luke 23:33–34

John 19:17–18

John 19:36–37

Acts 3:22

Romans 11:26–27

Romans 15:12

1 Peter 2:21–24

(*Also, see "Abortion," Christmas)

Prophesies About John, the Baptist

Isaiah 40:3–5
Malachi 3:1A
Malachi 4:5–6
Matthew 3
Mark 1:1–11

Luke 1:57–80
Luke 3:1–22
John 1:6–8
John 1:19–34

Prophesies About the Last Days

Psalms 2
Psalms 74
Psalms 83
Jeremiah 23:20–32
Daniel 12
Amos 8:11–14
Matthew 10:21–22
Matthew 16:1–3
Matthew 24
Mark 13:1–31
Luke 21
John 16:33

Romans 13:11
2 Thessalonians 2:3–4
1 Timothy 4:1–4
2 Timothy 3:1–9
2 Timothy 4:1–5
1 Peter 4:7
1 Peter 4:17
2 Peter 2
2 Peter 3:1–9
Jude 1
Revelation 6:1–8

Psalms of Christ

Psalms 2
Psalms 16:10
Psalms 22

Psalms 45
Psalms 69
Psalms 78:(1–4)

Psalms of David

2 Samuel 22
1 Chronicles 16:7–36

Psalms 51

Purgatory (?)

Psalms 65:1–3
Psalms 66:10–12
Psalms 79:5–9
Daniel 12:10

Zechariah 13:7–9
John 19:30
Romans 6:7–10
1 Corinthians 15:3

Galatians 2:21

Hebrews 1:1–3

Hebrews 2:9

Hebrews 9:11–28

Hebrews 10:1–10

1 Peter 1:6–7

2 Peter 1:9

We experience "purgatory" on Earth. The refinement, Zechariah discloses, is experienced through the trials, testing, suffering, and tough times we experience while living in this world. It's purpose is to produce perseverance, patience, character, and hope. (Romans 5:3–4.)

In certain scriptures in newer translations, purgatory is described as God providing atonement for our sins. In the Authorized King James Bible, the word for 'atone' or 'atonement' is the word "purge", in a few scriptures.

The Bible describes Jesus as the One who has atoned for, or purged, our sins, on the cross.

(Also, see, "Tough times.")

Purpose of Parables

Psalms 78:1–4

Isaiah 6:9–10

Matthew 13:10–17

Mark 4:10–12

Luke 8:9–10

Queen of Heaven*

Exodus 20:1–3

Deuteronomy 5:1–9

Jeremiah 7:15–18*

Jeremiah 44:(15–22)*

Question and Answer

Romans 10:14–21

Questions

Q1:   Regarding Adultery, (Mark 10:11–12), If we were once married to the law, and now, as the "bride", we are married to Christ (Revelation 21:(2, 9) has Christ committed "adultery"?

A: No. Romans 7:1–6

Q2: Where did I come from? What is my purpose on Earth?

A: Psalms 40:8   Matthew 7:21
    Psalms 102:18   1 Corinthians 10:31
    Isaiah 43:7   Revelation 4:11

Q3: What about tomorrow?

A: Proverbs 27:1   Philippians 3:13–14
    Matthew 6:25–34   James 4:13–17

Q4: What should I wear? (to church/synagogue)?

A: 1 Samuel 16:7   1 Thessalonians 5:22
    Matthew 6:25–33   1 Timothy 2:8–10
    Luke 12:22–28   1 Peter 5:5

Q5: What Does God Look Like?

A: Exodus 33:12–23   John 6:46
    Exodus 34   John 6:63
    Matthew 17:1–2   John 12:44–45
    Mark 9:2–3   John 14:7–11
    Luke 9:28–32   2 Corinthians 3:17A
    Luke 24:39   1 Timothy 6:13–16
    John 1:18   1 John 4:1–2
    John 4:24   Revelation 21:23
    John 5:37

Q6: Who Is/Are Israel?

A: Genesis 25:19–28   Psalms 105:6*
    Genesis 32:28   Matthew 3:9
    Genesis 35:9–10   Luke 3:8
    Genesis 49:1–28   John 4:22
    Psalms 22:23   Romans 2:28–29*
    Psalms 24:6*   Romans 9:6–13
    Psalms 53:6   Revelation 2:8–9
    Psalms 59:13   Revelation 3:7–9
    Psalms 75:9

(Also, see "God's Elect")

Q7: Why Has Jesus Not Returned Yet?

A:
Psalms 90:4	Luke 21:32–33
Lamentations 3:22–23	Acts 1:7
Joel 2:1	2 Peter 3
Matthew 24:34	Revelation 6:9–10

Q8: Who is Jesus?

A:
Genesis 22:8	2 Corinthians 5:21
Isaiah 9:6–7	Galatians 1:1–4
Isaiah 28:16	Philippians 2:5–11
Matthew 20:28	Colossians 1:15–18
Matthew 26:63–64	Colossians 2:8–9
Mark 2:13–20	1 Thessalonians 1:10
Mark 10:45	1 Timothy 1:15–16
John 1:1–16	1 Timothy 6:13–16
John 1:29–34	Hebrews Ch. 1–Ch. 2
John 1:48–49	Hebrews 4:15
John 3:16–18	Hebrews 5:1–11
John 4:39–42	Hebrews 7:20–28
John 5:22–27	Hebrews 12:2–3
John 6:66–69	1 John 2:1–2
John 10:22–30	1 John 3:5–8
John 16:28	Revelation 1:5–8
Acts 2:32	Revelation 1:18
Acts 4:10–12	Revelation 3:14
Acts 10:38–41	Revelation 5
Romans 6:8–10	Revelation 22:12–13
Romans 10:4	Revelation 22:16

(Also, see "Prophesies About Christ," "Jesus Is".)

Q9: If God does not change, (Malachi 3:6), why did he change the way we can escape Hell?

A: God originally designed two plans of salvation, from the foundation of the world, (Hebrews 4:3; 1 Peter 1:20; Revelation 13:8.)

In the history of the Old Testament, animal blood sacrifices were required as a type of fine to atone for sins. They were a design to appease God's anger for sin by burning, with a savory aroma that God enjoys smelling; just like we enjoy the smell of food cooking, (like bacon.)

The Old Testament history teaches a parable about New Testament doctrine. In Numbers 15:32–36, a man was caught picking up sticks on the Sabbath day, which violates God's law, that no work was to be done on the Sabbath; it is a day of rest and recuperation from 6 days of work. This act of work resulted in God's command for him to be stoned to death.

In one of the teachings of Harold Camping, this illustrated the attempt to work for our salvation, when God provides salvation for us, that we can rest and wait on Him to provide, (Genesis 22:8; Ephesians 2:8–9.)

God set up a salvation plan for a later time, that He would provide an Atonement for our sins. This is because people would sin and make their sacrifices, but their hearts would not be in it. There wouldn't be any sincere repentant motive behind the sacrifices. (Isaiah 1:10–15.)

The only ultimate heart-felt sacrifice for sin could only be provided by God Himself. This is why Jesus is metaphorically called the sacrificial Lamb of God, without any defects or blemishes.

Genesis 22:8	Hebrews 7
Micah 5:2	Hebrews 8
Ephesians 1:3–4	Hebrews 9:16–28
Hebrews 4:3A	Hebrews 10:1–10*
Hebrews 6:13–20	1 Peter 1:18–20

(Also, see "Prophesies About Christ," New Covenant, Work On Sundays)

The Roman Church teaches that we have to go through a period of refinement through fire before entering Heaven.

They call this "purgatory", or to be purged from all our sins, prior to entering Heaven. The scripture they use in this teaching is Zechariah 13:7–9, emphasizing verse 9. Purgatory sounds like an exact description of Hell; A.K.A., the lake of eternal fire, as described in Revelation.

One problem is that this is an Old Testament teaching (and probably metaphoric as well.) The Roman Church still adheres to certain Old Testament teachings that Christ took on Himself when He was nailed to the cross. (I.E., the priest burning incense on the alter; confessing sins to the priest, and being assigned acts of penance to counter-act the sins; when Christ is now our High Priest and enacted our penance on the cross.)

The reason the teaching of purgatory is probably metaphorical is because the Bible teaches that Jesus purged our sins for us. In newer "translations" of the Bible, words like 'atonement' are found that express God providing atonement for our sins. In the historical Authorized King James Bible, the act of God providing atonement for our sins is worded as Jesus purging our sins on the cross. (See "Purgatory")

So, we won't have to experience purgatory; Jesus already did it for us.

Q10: What does it mean to be created in God's image?

A: This is quite complex and probably has more details than any one can speculate. Part of God's image is eternal, sinless, and emotional. But according to the Bible, God's "image" does not include having physical descriptions; I.E., eyes hands, or wings. These descriptions are found to be metaphors. We possess certain traits of God.

Luke 24:39B   John 4:24

(Also, see "What Does God Look Like?")

Q11: Why Do Bad Things Happen to "Good" People?

Genesis Ch. 37– Ch. 45:5   Mark 10:17–22
Read Book of Job   Luke 9:23–27
Matthew 10:38–39   Luke 14:27
Matthew 16:24–25   John 9
Mark 8:34–35   2 Timothy 3:10–12

Q12: In the Old Testament, why are certain prophesies about Christ worded in a <u>past tense</u>; as if they already occurred, when Jesus did not come to Earth until the New Testament days?

I.E.: Hebrews 1:5   Psalms 118:22–23
        Hebrews 5:5   Isaiah 49:1–5
        Psalms 2:7   Hosea 11:1

A: According to the Bible, God already designed His plan for salvation before He created the universe. The reason for the past tenses of these prophesies is that Jesus, begotten into the physical world, was already planned, and what actually happened on the Earth was a demonstration of Gods plan, before the universe was created.

The Biblical expression, of this event taking place, is that these events <u>effectively</u> already took place "<u>before the foundation of the world</u>." Micah 5:2 describes this as "from everlasting." (See Question #9.)

The term "from everlasting" (Psalms 90:1–2, a song of Moses) means 'eternity past', which means God has no beginning; He always was. So, author, Richard Dawkins is partly right when he said God couldn't have just jumped into existence. God always existed. (See "God is Eternal.")

This is also what the "Jehovah's Witnesses" fail to understand, when they conclude that Jesus (allegedly) was a created being. (Psalms 2:7; Hebrews 1:5; Hebrews 5:5; John 1:1–2.)

Scriptures where you'll find the phrase "from the foundation of the world," or similar:

Micah 5:2–5   Hebrews 4:3
Matthew 13:34–35   Hebrews 9:26
Matthew 25:34   1 Peter 1:13–21
Luke 11:49–51   Revelation 13:8
Ephesians 1:3–4   Revelation 17:8

The scriptures pertaining to Jesus saying he was "first-born" and "today I have begotten you", the Jehovah's Witnesses use these scriptures to teach that Jesus was a created Being. But these scriptures are prophesies pertaining to Christ's incarnation into this world through the virgin, Mary. They are in a past tense because they are a written plan before God created creation, (before the foundation of the world.)

Quiet Spirit

Genesis 25:27	1 Peter 2:1–3
1 Thessalonians 4:11	1 Peter 3:3–4
2 Thessalonians 3:12	

Racism

1 Samuel 16:7	Acts 15:14–17
Joel 2:32	Romans 2:11
Amos 9:11–12	Romans 10:11–13
John 3:16	Galatians 3:26–29
John 4:9	Revelation 5:1–9
Acts 10:24–29	Revelation 7:9–10
Acts 10:34–35	Revelation 14:6–7
Acts 11:1–18	

(Also, see "Partiality," Second Greatest Commandment,"
"Golden Rule.")

Rainbows

Genesis 8:20–9:17

Rapture

Daniel 12	1 Corinthians 15:50–54
Matthew 13:24–43	Philippians 3:20–21
Matthew 13:47–50	Colossians 3:4
Matthew 16:27–28	1 Thessalonians 4:13–18
Mark 13:24–27	2 Thessalonians 2:1–4
Mark 14:60–62	2 Timothy 4:1
Luke 9:27	2 Timothy 4:8
Luke 17:20–37	James 5:7–8
John 5:28–29	1 Peter 5:4
John 6:39–54	1 John 2:28
John 12:48	1 John 3:2
1 Corinthians 4:5	Revelation 1:7
1 Corinthians 15:21–28	Revelation 14:15–16

Read the Bible

Psalms 1
Psalms 119:105
Ecclesiastes 12:11
Matthew 4:1–11
Matthew 6:11
John 5:39

John 6:66–69
Romans 10:17
Romans 12:2
Ephesians 6:17
1 Timothy 4:16

Reincarnation

Job 7:9–10
Ecclesiastes 12:6–8

2 Corinthians 5:6–10
Hebrews 9:27

Repentance/Conversion

Deuteronomy 30:1–10
1 Samuel 12:19–35
1 Samuel 15:24–25
2 Kings 22
2 Kings 23:1–25
2 Chronicles 7:1–22
   (13–15*)
2 Chronicles 15:1–2
2 Chronicles 30:8–9
Ezra Ch. 9–Ch. 10
Nehemiah 1
Nehemiah 9
Psalms 25:1
Psalms 51
Psalms 81:8–16
Psalms 85
Psalms 119:155
Psalms 144:11–15
Proverbs 28:13

Isaiah 44:21–22
Isaiah 55:6–7
Jeremiah 3:1–4:4
Jeremiah 36*
Jeremiah Ch. 42–Ch. 45
   Refusal
Daniel 9:1–19
Hosea 14
Joel 2:12–17
Jonah (Book)
Matthew 9:9–13
Matthew 18:3 (c)
Matthew 18:15–17 (Refusal)
Mark 2:13–17
Luke 5:27–32
Acts 3:19–21 (c)
Acts 17:30–31
2 Corinthians 6:14–18
Revelation 18:(4)

(* Change we can believe in.)
(c = Conversion)
(Seminaryathome.com; Dr. Duane Spencer)

Requests

1 Kings 3:1–15	Mark 10:46–52
1 Kings 4:29–31	Luke 11:5–13
2 Chronicles 1:1–12	Luke 12:29–32
Psalms 37:4	Luke 18:1–8
Psalms 86:6–7	John 2:1–11
Psalms 116:1–5	John 14:13–14
Psalms 142:1–2	John 15:7
Psalms 145:18–19	John 16:23–24
Isaiah 55:1–3	Philippians 4:6
Matthew 7:7–11	Hebrews 4:16
Matthew 20:20–23	James 4:1–5
Matthew 21:18–22	1 John 3:22
Mark 10:35–41	1 John 5:14–15

Requirements For Church Elders

Leviticus 21:1–15	1 Timothy 3:1–13
1 Timothy 2:11–14	Titus 1:1–16

(Also, see "Homosexuality")

Resurrection

Psalms 49:15	Luke 20:27–39
Ecclesiastes 12:7	Luke 24
Isaiah 26:19	John 5:24–29
Ezekiel 37:1–14	John 11:1–44
Daniel 12:1–3	John 20:1–29
Matthew 9:18–26	Acts 24:15
Matthew 22:23–32	1 Corinthians 15
Matthew 28:1–15	Philippians 3:20–21
Mark 5:21–43	Colossians 3:4
Mark 12:18–27	1 Thessalonians 4:15–18
Mark 16:1–13	2 Timothy 4:1
Luke 7:11–17	1 John 3:2
Luke 8:40–56	Revelation 11:7–12

Revenge

Genesis 4:8–15	Nahum 1:2–3
Leviticus 19:18	Luke 18:1–8
Deuteronomy 32:35	Luke 21:20–22
1 Samuel 24:12	Romans 12:19
Psalms 4:4	Romans 13:1–4
Psalms 94	1 Thessalonians 5:15
Proverbs 20:22	2 Thessalonians 1:6–10
Proverbs 24:17–18	2 Timothy 4:14
Proverbs 24:29	Hebrews 10:30–31
Isaiah 34:1–8	Jude 1:5–7

Rosary (Chanting)

Matthew 6:7–8A	Romans 1:25

Sacrifices

Psalms 4:5	Psalms 141:1–2
Psalms 50:7–15	Micah 6:6–8
Psalms 51:17	Romans 12:1
Psalms 69:29–33	Hebrews 13:15–16
Psalms 107:22	1 Peter 2:5
Psalms 116:17	

Salvation (Salvage)

Psalms 68:20	John 14:1–3
Psalms 119:155	John 17:3
Psalms 130:1–4	Acts 4:10–12
Proverbs 14:12	Acts 8:37
Proverbs 14:32	Acts 10:40–43
Proverbs 16:25	Acts 13:38–39
Isaiah 55:6–7	Romans 1:16–17
Isaiah 59:1	Romans 5:6–11
Joel 2:32	Romans 5:19
Jonah 2:9	Romans 8:1–5
Matthew 7:13–14	Romans 10:1–13
John 3:16–18	1 Corinthians 15:1–4
John 3:36	2 Corinthians 5:1
John 10:10	2 Corinthians 5:20–21

Galatians 4:1–7
Colossians 1:19–23
1 Thessalonians 5:9–10
1 Timothy 1:15–16

Hebrews 2:1–4 (3)
1 Peter 1:18–21 (18–19)
1 John 2:25
Revelation 21:1–7

Satan (the Devil) and Company
(Devil = Death, Evil*)

Genesis 3:1–15
Deuteronomy 30:15*
Job 1:6–12
Job 2:1–7
Isaiah 14:12–21
Ezekiel 28:1–19
Zechariah 3:1–2
Matthew 4:1–11
Luke 4:1–13
Luke 10:18
John 8:44

John 10:10A
Romans 16:20
2 Corinthians 11:13–15
Ephesians 2:1–3
2 Thessalonians 2:8–10
1 Peter 5:8–9
2 Peter 2:4
1 John 3:8
Jude 1:6
Revelation 12:1–12

Scoffers
(Complainers, Scorners, Skeptics)

Proverbs 13:1
Proverbs 14:6
Proverbs 15:12
Proverbs 21:21

Proverbs 22:10
Proverbs 29:8
Mark 15:1–32
2 Peter 3:8–9

Seeing is Believing

Exodus 33:18–Ch. 34
Deuteronomy 11:7
Psalms 107:23–43
Matthew 12:38–40
Matthew 28
Mark 16
Luke 24
John 4:46–54 (48)
John 6:30–36
John 7:20–23

John 10:22–32
John 11:1–45
John 12:15–17
John 19:35
John Ch. 20–Ch. 21
Acts 2:1–3:11
1 Corinthians 15:1–17
2 Corinthians 4:18
Hebrews 11:1
2 Peter 1:16–19

(Also, see "Faith")

Self Defense

Exodus 22:2

Self Denial

Isaiah 53:3–6
Mark 8:34–36
Mark 10:42–45
Luke 9:23–27
Luke 9:57–62

Luke 14:25–33
John 15:13
Acts 20:35
1 Corinthians 10:12
2 Corinthians 9:6–9

Self Esteem

Romans 12:3
1 Corinthians 4:6–7

1 Peter 5:5

(Also, see "Pride", "Humility")

Selling the Gospel

Matthew 10:8
1 Corinthians 9:16–18

2 Corinthians 2:17
2 Corinthians 11:7

Separation of Church and State

Leviticus 26
Numbers 14:42–43
Numbers 32:11–15
Deuteronomy 11:13–28
Deuteronomy 28
Judges 2:11–3:6
1 Kings 11
2 Chronicles 7:12–22*
Ezra 7:24*
Ezra 8:21–23
Ezra Ch. 9–Ch. 10
Nehemiah 1:4–11
Nehemiah 13
Psalms 2
Psalms 21

Psalms 22:18
   (Rejecting God)
Psalms 33:10–12
Psalms Ch. 77–Ch. 78
Psalms 81:(8–16)
Psalms 83
Psalms Ch. 102– Ch. 107
Psalms 108:10–13
Psalms 115
Psalms 119:126
Psalms 127:1
Psalms 144
Proverbs 14:34
Proverbs 19:21
Isaiah 5:13–14

Isaiah 19:(3–4)
Isaiah 33:6
Isaiah 46:(10–11)
Jeremiah 2:26–28
Jeremiah 10:17–22
Jeremiah 11:9–14
Jeremiah Ch. 16–Ch. 22
Jeremiah 31:16–19
Jeremiah 32:(33–34)
Jeremiah 36
Jeremiah 44
Jeremiah 50:6–7

Lamentations (2)
Ezekiel 23:(22–30)
Hosea (Book)
Jonah (Book)
Nahum (Book)
Malachi 2:1–9
Luke 19:11–27 (14, 27)
Acts 7:37–43 (39)
Romans 1:18–32
Romans 13:1–7
Hebrews 3:12
Hebrews 10:38

(Also, see "Repentance", "Sin")
(Government − God = Disaster)

Sermon on the Mount

Matthew Ch. 5–Ch. 7   Luke 6:20–49

Service

Psalms 37:21
Psalms 112:5
Proverbs 11:25
Proverbs 21:13
Proverbs 22:9
Proverbs 25:21–22
Matthew 7:12
Matthew 10:1–15
Matthew 20:25–28
Matthew 21:28–31A
Mark 1:29–31
Mark 8:34–35
Mark 9:30–32
Mark 10:17–22
Mark 10:42–45
Luke 4:38–39

Luke 6:27–35
Luke 10:38–42
Luke 14:12–14
John 12:26
John 13:1–17
Acts 20:35
Romans 12:1–13
1 Corinthians 7:32–35
2 Corinthians 9:6–7
Galatians 5:13–14
Philippians 2:5–8
Philippians 2:14–15
Titus 3:14
James 2:15–16
1 John 3:17

Seven Hated Sins

Proverbs 6:16–19

Sex With Animals

Exodus 20:14
Exodus 22:19
Leviticus 18:23

Leviticus 20:15–16
Deuteronomy 27:21
Jude 1:(5–7)

Shoplifting (*)

Exodus 20:15
Deuteronomy 5:19
Proverbs 6:30–31*

Proverbs 28:21*
Matthew 5:7*

Show Off, Do Not

Matthew 5:13–16
Matthew 6:1–6

Matthew 6:16–18
(Also, see Hypocrisy)

Sin

Leviticus 26
Numbers 32:11–15
Numbers 32:20–23
Deuteronomy 18:9–14
Deuteronomy 27:14–26
1 Samuel 15:22–23
2 Kings 14:6
2 Kings 21:1–18
2 Chronicles 6:36–40
2 Chronicles 24:20
2 Chronicles 25:4
2 Chronicles 33:1–9
Ezra Ch. 9–Ch. 10
Psalms 14:1–3
Psalms 37:1–8
Psalms 58:1–5
Psalms 90:7–8
Psalms 92:7–9

Psalms 101
Psalms 119:136
Psalms 119:165
Psalms 143:1–2
Proverbs 10:16
Proverbs 14:9
Proverbs 14:11
Proverbs 17:12
Proverbs 26:11
Proverbs 28:9
Proverbs 28:13
Proverbs 29:24
Ecclesiastes 8:11
Isaiah 1
Isaiah 30:1
Isaiah 59:1–3
Jeremiah Ch. 7–Ch. 9
Jeremiah 10:24

Jeremiah 11
Jeremiah Ch. 16–Ch. 22
Ezekiel 18:10–18
Matthew 7:21–23
Matthew 9:9–13
Matthew 15:8–20
Matthew 26:26–28
Mark 2:13–17
Mark 7:14–23
Luke 5:27–32
John 8:32–35
Romans 1:18–32
Romans 3:9–23
Romans 5:8
Romans Ch. 6–Ch. 7
Romans 12:2
Romans 13:13–14
Romans 14:23
1 Corinthians 5:9–13
1 Corinthians 6:9–10
1 Corinthians 10:1–13
Galatians 5:16–21

Ephesians 5:5–14
Colossians 3:5–10
1 Thessalonians 5:22
1 Timothy 1:8–11
1 Timothy 6:9–10
James 1:13–15
James 2:10
James 4:17
1 Peter 2:11–12
1 Peter 4:1–5
1 Peter 5:8–9
2 Peter 2
1 John 1:5–10
1 John 2:12
1 John 2:16
1 John 3:4
1 John 3:8
1 John 5:17
3 John 1:11
Jude 1:5–19
Revelation 21:1–8
Revelation 22:14–15

Sins Against Children

Matthew 18:1–7
Mark 9:42

Luke 17:1–2

Slander
(Backbiting, Gossip, Rumors, Scandal)

Exodus 20:16
Exodus 23:1
Leviticus 19:16
Psalms 15:1–3
Psalms 34:13
Psalms 101:5

Psalms 140:11
Proverbs 10:18
Proverbs 20:19
Proverbs 26:20
1 Timothy 5:11–13

Slavery/Freedom

John 8:32–36	Romans 6:22
Romans 6:6–7	Galatians 5:1

(Also, see "Liberty")

Sorcery
(Mediums, Psychics, Soothsayers, Witchcraft)

Exodus 22:18	1 Samuel 28
Leviticus 19:31	2 Chronicles 33:1–6
Leviticus 20:6	Acts 13:6–11
Leviticus 20:27	Acts 16:16–19
Deuteronomy 18:9–12	Galatians 5:19–20
1 Samuel 15:22–23	

Spiritual Bread

Exodus 16:1–17:7	Luke 4:3–4
Deuteronomy 8:3	Luke 11:3
Isaiah 55:1–3	Luke 12:1
Matthew 4:1–4	Luke 22:19
Matthew 6:11	John 6:22–63
Matthew 16:5–12	John 9:31
Matthew 26:26	1 Corinthians 10:1–4
Mark 8:1–8	1 Corinthians 10:17
Mark 14:22	

Spiritual Water

Exodus 17:1–6	John 6:32–35
Numbers 20:1–11	John 7:37–38
Psalms 78:12–16	1 Corinthians 10:1–4
Psalms 105:41	Revelation 21:6
Luke 16:19–24	Revelation 22:1
John 4:1–15	Revelation 22:17

(Water = Salvation. The water of life comes from God, the Rock.
Also, see "God is the Rock.")

Spiritually Minded

Romans 8:1–17

    (Also, see "Read the Bible", "Double Minded.")

Status of the "Heart"

Proverbs 12:25   Proverbs 18:14
Proverbs 15:4   Proverbs 23:7
Proverbs 15:14   Jeremiah 17:9
Proverbs 17:22   Mark 7:20–23

Statute of Limitations

Deuteronomy 15:1–4

Steeling, Theft, Burglary (Coveting)

Exodus 20:15   Proverbs 20:21
Exodus 20:17   Proverbs 21:6
Exodus 22:2   Proverbs 28:21
Leviticus 19:11   Proverbs 29:24
Leviticus 19:13   Matthew 5:40
Deuteronomy 5:19   Luke 6:29
Proverbs 6:30–31   1 Corinthians 6:9–10

    (Also, see "Coveting", "Golden Rule", "Second Greatest
Commandment", "Self Denial.")

Stewardship/Management

Matthew 25:14–30   Luke 19:20–26
Luke 16:1–13   1 Corinthians 4:1–2

Success

John 17:4   1 Corinthians 3:5–7
John 19:30

Suicide/Death Wish

Exodus 20:13
Deuteronomy 5:17
Job 3:11

2 Corinthians 1:1–10
2 Corinthians 4:6–18
Philippians 1:23–24

(Also, see "Tough Times")

Sunday Sabbath

Exodus 20:8
Exodus 31:12–18
Leviticus 19:3
Leviticus 23:3
Leviticus 25:1–7
Deuteronomy 5:12–14
Isaiah 1:13
Isaiah 58:13–14
Matthew 12:1–14
Matthew 28
Mark 2:23–28

Mark 3:1–6
Mark 16:9–11
Luke 6:1–11
Luke 24
John 5:1–17
John 20
Acts 20:7
Romans 14:5–8
1 Corinthians 16:2
Colossians 2:16–17

Tattoos/Body Piercings/Self Mutilation

Leviticus 19:28
1 Corinthians 3:16–17

1 Corinthians 10:31

Temptation

Genesis 3
2 Samuel Ch. 11–Ch. 12
Proverbs 7:6–27
Matthew 4:1–11
Matthew 6:13A
Matthew 26:41
Mark 14:38
Luke 4:1–13

Luke 8:11–13
Luke 22:39–46
1 Corinthians 10:12–13
Hebrews 2:16–18
Hebrews 4:15–16
James 1:12–16
2 Peter 2:9

(Seminaryathome.com; Dr. Duane Spencer, keyword 'Prove')

10 Commandments

Exodus 20:1–17	Luke 18:18–27
Deuteronomy 5:1–22	Romans 13:8–10

Thankfulness/Thanksgiving

Psalms 50:14	1 Corinthians 1:1–4
Psalms 69:29–33	2 Corinthians 4:15
Psalms 92:1	2 Corinthians 9:10–15
Psalms 100:4–5	Ephesians 5:3–4
Psalms 106:1	Ephesians 5:20
Psalms 107:15	Philippians 1:1–3
Psalms 107:22	Philippians 4:6
Psalms 116:16–17	Colossians 1:1–3
Psalms 118	Colossians 3:17
Psalms 119:62	1 Thessalonians 1:1–3
Psalms 136	1 Thessalonians 2:13
Psalms 140:13	1 Thessalonians 5:18
Psalms 147:7	2 Thessalonians 1:1–3
Matthew 15:36	2 Timothy 1:1–3
Luke 17:11–19	Hebrews 13:15
John 6:11	Revelation 7:11–12
Acts 27:35	

(Also, see "Prayer")

Tithing (¹⁄₁₀)

Genesis 14:18–20	Malachi 3:8–12
Genesis 28:22	Matthew 23:23
Numbers 18:26–28	Luke 6:38
Deuteronomy 14:22–29	Luke 11:42
Deuteronomy 26:12–13	Luke 18:9–14
2 Chronicles 31:5–6	Luke 21:1–4
Nehemiah 10:37	Acts 20:35
Nehemiah 12:44	2 Corinthians 9:6–15
Nehemiah 13:5–12	Hebrews 7:1–2

"Tongues"

1 Corinthians 14:1–25

Tough Times, Trials, Testing, Suffering

Genesis Ch. 37–Ch. 50
Deuteronomy 8:5
Deuteronomy 13:1–5
Judges 10
Job (Book)
Psalms 3
Psalms 7:8–11
Psalms 23
Psalms 25:15–18
Psalms 34:17–19
Psalms 46:1–3
Psalms 77
Psalms 118:18
Psalms 119:71
Proverbs 3:11–12
Proverbs 3:25–26
Proverbs 12:1
Proverbs 13:18
Proverbs 15:10
Isaiah 41:14–16
Matthew 5:10
Matthew 10:28
Matthew 11:28–30
Luke 12:42–48
John 16:33
Acts 14:21–22
Acts 27:23–25

Romans 5:3–5
Romans 8:16–18
Romans 8:28–29
1 Corinthians 4:3–4
1 Corinthians 11:32
2 Corinthians 1:1–10
2 Corinthians 4:8–10
2 Corinthians 6:1–10
2 Corinthians 7:1–7
2 Corinthians 11:24–28
2 Corinthians 12:7–10
Philippians 1:12–14
Philippians 1:29–30
1 Thessalonians 2:4
1 Thessalonians 5:18
2 Timothy 2:3
2 Timothy 3:12–13
Hebrews 6:13–15
Hebrews 12:5–11
James 1:1–4
James 5:10–11
1 Peter 1:6–7
1 Peter 2:20–25
1 Peter 3:14–18
1 Peter 4:12–19
2 Peter 1:1–9
Revelation 3:19

Traditions

Matthew 15:1–14
Mark 7:1–13
Colossians 2:8

2 Thessalonians 2:15
2 Thessalonians 3:6
1 Peter 1:18–19

Tribulation/Abomination of Desolation

Deuteronomy 4:28–31
Judges 10:6–18
1 Samuel 26:24
Daniel 12
Matthew 13:18–21
Matthew 24:15–29
Mark 13:14–29
Luke 21:20–28
John 16:33
Acts 14:21–22
Romans 2:1–10
Romans 5:1–4

Romans 8:35–39
Romans 12:9–13
2 Corinthians 1:3–4
2 Corinthians 7:1–4
1 Thessalonians 3:1–4
2 Thessalonians 1:6
1 Peter 4:17
Revelation 1:9
Revelation 2:8–10
Revelation 2:18–23
Revelation 7:9–14

Trinity (Tri-unity; 3 in 1)

Genesis 1:26–27
Genesis 3:22–23A
Genesis 11:6–7
Exodus 3:14
Isaiah 6:8
Isaiah 9:6
Matthew 3:16–17
Matthew 28:19–20
Mark 12:29–32
John 1:1–2
John 3:11
John 5:16–47
John 6:27
John 8:58
John 10:30
John 14:7–11
John 14:16–17

John 14:26
John 15:26
John 16:7–8
John 17:1–5
1 Corinthians 12:3
1 Corinthians 15:47
Ephesians 4:1–6
Philippians 2:11
Colossians 1:13–19
Colossians 2:1–10
1 Thessalonians 1:1–10
1 Peter 1:1–2
1 John 1:1–3
1 John 5:5–8
Revelation 1:17–18
Revelation 22:13
Revelation 22:16

(Also, see "God is . . .")

The Unknown God

John 4:19–22

Acts 17:22–34

The Unpardonable Sin

Mark 3:20–30

Victory

Joshua 6:1–27   1 Corinthians 15:54–57
Judges 12:1–3   1 John 5:4

Virgin Birth of Christ

Isaiah 7:14   Luke 1:26–38
Matthew 1:18–23

Virgin Mary, a Perpetual Virgin (?)
(Never Had Sex With Her Husband)

Matthew 1:18–25 (25)   John 7:1–5 (5)
Matthew 13:53–56

In an issue of a Lancaster, Pennsylvania newspaper, around Christmas, 2011, a Roman Catholic columnist defended the Roman Church's doctrine of Mary being a continual virgin up to her death, even though the Bible clearly states that Mary had other children after Jesus was born into this world. But Matthew 1:25 and Luke 2:7 state that Jesus was Mary's firstborn Son; "firstborn", indicating that other offspring of Mary followed <u>after</u> Jesus was born.

However, this Roman Catholic columnist continued to defend this Roman fable by speculating that Mary's other children were allegedly fathered by Joseph in a previous marriage, possibly he was divorced.

But besides the Bible declaring that Jesus was Mary's first born child, the Bible also declares that "God HATES divorce", Malachi 2:16. Since God hates divorce, and divorce is a sin, and re-marriage after divorce is adultery, it is a more logical conclusion that God would choose a more reputable husband for Mary, to be Jesus step-father.

This new-found doctrine would be called hear-say. I believe "hear-say" is where we get the word heresy.(?) Heresy is any doctrine that contradicts what the Bible teaches, and the Roman Church seems to teach a significant amount of it, as outlined in other topics, and described by the late Doctor Duane Spencer (Seminaryathome.com).

War

Exodus 15:3
Numbers 10:9
Deuteronomy 20
Joshua 6
Judges 1:1–4
1 Samuel 17
1 Chronicles 5:21–22
2 Chronicles 20:1–30
2 Chronicles 32:1–23
Psalms 108:11–13
Psalms 120:6–7

Proverbs 20:18
Proverbs 21:31
Ecclesiastes 3:8
Isaiah 40:1–2
Matthew 24:6
2 Corinthians 10:1–6
Galatians 5:16–17
Ephesians 6:10–20
Revelation 12:7
Revelation 19:11

Wealth

Deuteronomy 8:14–18
Job 1:1–22
Job 31:24–28
Job 42
Psalms 19:7–11
Psalms 37:(16–20)
Psalms 49:6–20
Psalms 52
Psalms 62:10
Psalms 73
Psalms 112:1–3
Psalms 119:17
Psalms 119:127–128
Proverbs 1:1–19
Proverbs 11:4
Proverbs 11:28
Proverbs 13:7
Proverbs 13:11
Proverbs 13:22
Proverbs 15:16

Proverbs 16:8
Proverbs 19:4
Proverbs 20:21
Proverbs 21:6
Proverbs 22:2
Proverbs 22:4
Proverbs 23:4–5
Proverbs 27:23–24
Proverbs 28:6
Proverbs 28:11
Proverbs 28:20
Proverbs 28:22
Proverbs 30:7–9*
Ecclesiastes 5:10–11
Jeremiah 9:23–24
Jeremiah 17:11
Hosea 13
Zephaniah 1:14–18
Matthew 6:19–34
Matthew 16:26

Matthew 19:16–26
Mark 10:17–27
Luke 12:13–24
Luke 12:48B
Luke 18:18–27
John 3:27
2 Corinthians 8:9
Philippians 3:7–8

Colossians 3:1–2
1 Timothy 6:17–19
Hebrews 10:34
James 1:5–6
James 1:9–11
James 5:1–6
Revelation 21:9–27

We're All God's Children (?)

Malachi 1:1–3
Matthew 13:24–30
Matthew 13:36–43
John 3:7–8

John 8:37–47
Acts 13:4–10
1 John 3:10–15

Which Way?

Joshua 24:15
Psalms 23:1–3
Psalms 37:34
Psalms 62:1–7
Proverbs 3:5–8
Proverbs 12:28
Proverbs 14:12

Proverbs 16:25
Matthew 7:13–14
Luke 13:23–28
John 8:30–31
John 10:1–9
John 14:1–6

Wisdom and Knowledge (of God and His Law)

Exodus 28:3
Exodus 36:1–2
1 Kings Ch. 3–Ch. 4
1 Kings 5:12
1 Kings 7:13–14
1 Kings 10:1–8
1 Kings 10:23–24
1 Kings 11:41
2 Chronicles 1:1–12
2 Chronicles 9:1–23
Job 15:1–3
Job 21:22
Psalms 94:10

Psalms 139:6
Proverbs 1:7
Proverbs 1:22
Proverbs 2
Proverbs 8:10
Proverbs 10:14
Proverbs 12:1
Proverbs 12:23
Proverbs 15:2
Proverbs 17:27
Proverbs 18:15
Proverbs 22:17–19
Ecclesiastes 1:16–18

Ecclesiastes 2:21–26
Ecclesiastes 7:12
Ecclesiastes 9:10
Ecclesiastes 12:9–12
Isaiah 2:3
Isaiah 5:13
Isaiah 11:1–9
Isaiah 33:6
Isaiah 40:12–14
Isaiah 44:24–25
Isaiah 45:20
Isaiah 47:10–11
Jeremiah 3:14–15
Jeremiah 4:22
Jeremiah 10:14–16
Jeremiah 51:17–19
Daniel 2:20–21

Hosea 4:1–6
Hosea 6:6
Luke 16:1–8
Romans 1:14–23
Romans 11:25
Romans 12:16
Romans 15:4
1 Corinthians 1:17–30
1 Corinthians 2:1–13
1 Corinthians 3:19–20
1 Corinthians 8:1–2
Colossians 2:1–3
1 Timothy 6:20–21
James 1:5–6
James 3:13–17
Revelation 13:18

Witness (Noun, Verb)

Isaiah 43:10–13
Isaiah 44:8–9
Isaiah 52:7
Jeremiah 1:1–9
John 12:37–41
Acts 1:7–8
Acts 2:32
Acts 3:11–15
Acts 5:30–32
Acts 10:34–43

Romans 2:17–20
Romans 10:14–15
1 Corinthians 1:18
1 Corinthians 3:5–8
2 Corinthians 5:11
2 Timothy 4:1–5
Philemon 1:4–7 (6)
2 Peter 1:16–18
Revelation 11:1–14

The Word of God is Like a Sword

Ephesians 6:17
Hebrews 4:12
James 3:1–12

Revelation 1:16
Revelation 2:12–16
Revelation 19:15–16

Work On Sundays (New Testament Sabbath)

Genesis 2:2–3
Exodus 12:16
Exodus 20:8–11
Exodus 23:12
Exodus 31:14–17
Exodus 34:21
Exodus 35:1–3
Leviticus 16:29–31
Leviticus 23:3

Matthew 12:9–14
Mark 3:1–6
Luke 6:6–11
Luke 13:10–17
Luke 14:1–6
John 5:1–18
John 7:19–24
John 9:1–34

(Also, see Question #9)

The World is Passing Away

Proverbs 23:17–18
Isaiah 40:8
Matthew 24:35
Mark 13:31

Luke 21:33
1 Corinthians 7:29–31
1 John 2:17
Revelation 21:4

Worldliness

Matthew 4:1–11
Matthew 15:17–20
Mark 7:1–23
Mark 8:36
John 7:7
John 8:23
John 15:18–19
Romans 12:2
Romans 13:13–14

Galatians 5:19–21
Philippians 4:8
Colossians 3:1–10
James 4:1–4
1 Peter 4:3
1 John 2:15–17
Revelation 21:8
Revelation 22:14–15

You Are a Temple

John 2:18–22
1 Corinthians 3:16–17
1 Corinthians 6:15–20

1 Corinthians 9:27
2 Corinthians 6:14–18 (16)

You Talk Too Much

Proverbs 10:19
Proverbs 13:3
Proverbs 17:27–28
Proverbs 29:11
Proverbs 29:20
Matthew 26:62–64

Mark 14:60–62
Luke 23:8–9
John 19:8–9
2 Corinthians 12:6–10
James 1:19
James 3:5–12

Zion

2 Samuel 5:6–9
2 Kings 19:31
2 Chronicles 5:2
Psalms 2:6
Psalms 9:11
Psalms 48:1–3
Psalms 69:35
Psalms 74:1–2
Psalms 76:1–2
Psalms 87:1–2

Psalms 125:1
Psalms 132:13–14
Psalms 134:3
Isaiah 18:7
Isaiah 28:16
Isaiah 59:20
Romans 11:26–27
Hebrews 12:22
1 Peter 2:4–6
Revelation 14:1

Guide Through Handel's Messiah

1. Overture
2. Isaiah 40:1–3
3. Isaiah 40:4
4. Isaiah 40:5
5. Haggai 2:6–7, Malachi 3:1; (Hebrews 12:25–28)
6. Malachi 3:2
7. Malachi 3:3
8. Matthew 1:23 (Isaiah 7:14)
9. Isaiah 40:9, Isaiah 60:1
10. Isaiah 60:2–3
11. Isaiah 9:2
12. Isaiah 9:6
13. Pastoral symphony
14. Luke 2:8–9
15. Luke 2:10
16. Luke 2:13
17. Luke 2:14
18. Zechariah 9:9–10
19. Isaiah 35:5–6
20. Isaiah 40:11, Matthew 11:28–29
21. Matthew 11:30
22. John 1:29
23. Isaiah 53:3, Lamentations 3:30
24. Isaiah 53:4–5A
25. Isaiah 53:5B
26. Isaiah 53:6
27. Psalms 22:7
28. Psalms 22:8 (Matthew 27:43)
29. Psalms 69:20
30. Lamentations 1:12
31. Isaiah 53:8
32. Psalms 16:10
33. Psalms 24:7–10
34. Hebrews 1:5
35. Hebrews 1:6
36. Psalms 68:18
37. Psalms 68:11
38. Romans 10:15 (Isaiah 52:7)

39. Romans 10:18
40. Psalms 2:1–2
41. Psalms 2:3
42. Psalms 2:4
43. Psalms 2:9 (Rev. 2:27)
44. *Revelation 19:6, Revelation 11:15, Revelation 19:16
45. Job 19:25–26, 1 Corinthians 15:20
46. 1 Corinthians 15:21–22
47. 1 Corinthians 15:51–52A
48. 1 Corinthians 15:52B–53
49. 1 Corinthians 15:54
50. 1 Corinthians 15:55–56
51. 1 Corinthians 15:57
52. Romans 8:31,33,34
53. Revelation 5:12–13 Amen

Abortion

Abortion is one of those moral and social controversies because it involves religion and peoples selfishness and how Gods word is involved.

I have heard that the process of an abortion is similar to putting a baby into a blender. The blender is shoved into the woman's womb and chops up the infant.

But, the question is, what does Gods word constitute as a legitimate human life? Most would say it is when the baby exits the womb. Others may say it is at the time of conception or one stage of gestation.

The people who say it is when birth takes place are probably the ones who do not want to look at the baby it involves. So, technical devices, like ultra sound are being used to get a look at a living life form in the womb and how it behaves.

Other pro-choice people say it is a matter of ownership; I.E. "It's my body, I'll do what I want with it". (See "You are a Temple") The next question is, what are they referring to as their body? If they are implying the baby is their body, they are wrong. It may be the mother's flesh and blood, but the baby's body belongs to the baby and the soul that dwells in it. There is an individual, legitimate human being in the womb, and I hope to shed some Godly, Biblical light on why this is so.

Genesis 2:7 says, "The Lord God formed man out of the dust of the ground, breathed into his nostrils the breath of life, and man became a living soul."

In the womb, the sperm and egg are united, and the process of a growing baby is alive and active.

In Psalms 5:15, David said, "I was brought fourth in iniquity, and in sin did my mother conceive me." Notice that David does not say 'conceived my body' he says conceived <u>him</u>. God already has a soul, or spirit, created to possess the embryo in the womb.

But what about rape, incest or protecting the mother's life, if a pregnancy endangers her life? Once again, remember that an embryo is its own life form with its own soul. That baby is not the one deserving death for sexual sins—the parents are! So how about saving the baby, stone the unmarried or incestuous father to death, and as soon as the baby is born, stone the mother to death, if she was a voluntary participant in the sin. But the baby is innocent of that sin, let <u>IT</u> live!

So, what about protecting the mother's life? There are specialists who work in this issue. One is known as The Deborah Heart and Lung Center, in Pemberton, New Jersey. Both lives should be saved.

Let us look, in the Bible, at some examples of rape and incest. (Let's first remember that rape and incest are sins.)

First, if we look at Genesis chapter 16, we could change Hagar's scenario to a incident of rape, God disclosed to Hagar a purpose for her babies life. And so is true for any baby conceived, regardless of the moral mode of conception.

Second, Genesis Chapter 17, a woman near 100 years old is going to have a baby. This could put the mother's life in danger, or the baby's life or physical well being. But once again, God discloses his purpose for that baby.

Third, Genesis 19:30–38, an incident of incest. In spite of this disgusting sin, these two daughters decide they have no other choice than the method they chose to retain the linage of their father. And once again, the two sons conceived by incest had a purpose for their lives.

In conclusion, we are not to give a death sentence for babies who are not conceived in the ways that we do not feel are traditionally and morally acceptable; those babies did not sin.

Recently, a celebrity in the secular music realm had a baby (unmarried) but it was reported that her boyfriend left her because he did not want the baby. Now that is immaturity!!

God will have a purpose for every life that is conceived, unless he allows one to die at birth, but even that untimely death has a purpose.

The most vivid example to make us think is the Christmas event. The virgin Mary possessed the Son of God in her womb, who would be the Savior of His people from their sins.

Suppose Mary was to go to Planned Parenthood to seek an abortion. She would have murdered the Son of God (God in the flesh), Who has been alive since eternity.

But all of these scenarios are still a bit vague in defining when a human life begins. However, there is a passage of scripture that gives us God's bedrock answer to this question.

In a few places in the Bible, blood is used to typify life and/or death. In Genesis Chapter 4, Cain murdered his brother Abel. God said to Cain, "What have you done?! The voice of your brothers blood cries to me from the ground!"

In Proverbs chapter 6, God declares seven hated sins. One of them is murder. But God words this sin as "hands that shed innocent blood," or forcing an innocent person to shed his life.

In Hebrews chapter 9, God declares, through the apostle, "Without the shedding of blood, there is no remission" (of sins.)

So, when does a human life begin? In <u>Leviticus chapter 17</u>, in the teaching of animal sacrifices, God declares that "the life of ALL flesh is in the blood."

So, the question is, after the male's seed and the female's egg unite, how long does it take for the blood to begin flowing into the tiny body? That's when an embryo or fetus is a Biblically constitutional living person.

Age of Accountability

This became an issue with a former pen pal (and still a friend),—a lady with active maternal instincts. And there are other similar ladies out there who may be asking this question:

If the Bible (God's Word) says we need to accept Jesus Christ into our hearts; and if we don't, we'll go to Hell, what happens to babies who are still-born, and children who die before they're aware of their existence, or those who are aware, and do not understand the concepts of good and evil?

I, previously, wrote a commentary about this issue a few years ago, but I was omitting it because of insufficient research, and I had not planed on publishing anything about this question. But, earlier this year, (2012), (14 years after beginning this project,) I was surveying the first five books of the Bible, for more education to add to this book. In one of those surveys, God finally led me to a scripture that gives a direct answer to this question.

At first, years earlier, some scriptures were brought to my attention by a few pastors: Matthew 18:14, Acts 7:19, and Romans 9:6–26. Although these scriptures seem to imply this topic, none of them give a direct answer about it. But in February of this year (2012), the Lord led me to Deuteronomy 1:39;

When Moses was debriefing Israel before he was to die, and before Israel was to enter the promised land, Moses said, through inspiration of the Holy Ghost, "Your little ones and your children, who you say will be victims, who today have no knowledge of good or evil, they shall enter in there; to them I will give it and they shall possess it."

One thing to remember in Bible Study is that the Bible contains prophesies and parables. Some prophesies pertain to upcoming events. One of these combinations is Genesis 21:8. This parabolic prophesy implies the impending incarnate arrival of Jesus into this world, the Lamb of God.

In like manner, I believe Deuteronomy 1:39, is parabolic of the age of accountability to certain children going to Heaven.

I also believe we also have to go back in scripture and tie this in with Genesis chapter 2, verse 8, through chapter 3, verse 24.

Adam and Eve were, at first, not aware of good or evil. They could be compared to new-born babies, which they were, in a way, since they were newly created beings (Genesis 2:7.) But, just like growing children, Adam and Eve eventually learned good and evil. They discovered these concepts after eating from the tree of the knowledge of good and evil, which God told them not to do. (See, "Temptation.")

Before they ate of that tree, Adam and Eve were spiritually alive, not knowing good or evil. But after they ate of it, they were spiritually dead, knowing good and evil.

Such is the same of children;

They are spiritually alive in their early days, unaware of good or evil. But, at a certain point in our lives, we die, spiritually, and are bound for Hell, in which Jesus died in our place. Living a "good" life (salvation by works, Eph. 2:8–10) will not reconcile us to God. Only by the shedding of Christ's blood on the cross, can we be reconciled to God. (Romans 5:6–11)

In other research, this also is linked to the Jewish rituals of the Bar Mitzvah for boys, and Bat Mitzvah for girls. These rituals are based on Jewish teachings of when boys and girls become of age where they are accountable for their actions; 12 years old for girls, and 13 years old for boys.

But no where in the Bible does it give an actual age of accountability. We are better off letting God worry about that.

"Contemporary" Worship

What is this trend called "Contemporary" worship? I'll have to agree with conservative pastors, that this is a worldly flavor added to a Godly environment. Some members of the younger generation don't like the sound of slow-moving music, particularly in the hymns. They find it easier to sing with faster music. This is because slower singing requires talent to hold notes longer, besides other possible factors.

I admit I tend to think that way myself. But I have enough sense to appreciate the consistent worship in the old hymns. Contemporary lyrics have vague composition.

One preacher advised, if you don't know how to give praise to God, read the praises in the Bible to God. I'm sorry to admit that the Lord's model prayer has become somewhat dull to me. (But I do pray that prayer when I feel there's a practical need to.) So, lately, I've switched to a different scripture to offer praise to God; Psalms 90:1–2.

A lot of new "talent" gives vague praise to God; I.E., "Praise You God, I praise You." The question is, what do you praise God about?

We all enjoy praise from our family, and friends, and employers. I.E., "You're a good worker," "that was good." But we especially enjoy praise for a specific reason. I.E., "You did a good job on that project"; "that's a beautiful dress you made!"

In the same way, God enjoys specific praise and thanks; Psalms 90:1–2.

The hymns also contain other forms of edification for the people who value them; I.E., "Showers of Blessing", Ezekiel 34:26; "Holy Holy Holy", Revelation 4:8; Amazing Grace, Ephesians 2:4–9.

And, in some hymns, you'll find different doctrinal scriptures combined in one hymn. In the hymns, you'll find Bible doctrine lyrics that provide education, edification (soul food), hope, and elaborate praise.

One younger generation Christian told me, "God should keep up with the changing times." God knew how the times would change before the world was created. (This might also be what homosexuals think.) (Daniel 7:23–28(25)). But God says in His word, in Malachi 3:6A, "I Am the Lord, I do not change." This is to say that God's nature doesn't change; His character doesn't change; His law doesn't change; His value system doesn't change; and His mercy doesn't change, Psalms 136.

So, besides reading your Bible, take some time to read a hymnal, and learn to appreciate God's preferred method of worship.

Divorce/Annulment and Remarriage

One Biblical controversy is what is taught about divorce and remarriage. The scripture of controversy is Matthew 5:32, Jesus said, "Whoever divorces his wife for any reason, except sexual immorality causes her to commit adultery; and whoever marries a woman who is divorced commits adultery."

Paul advises us to compare scripture with scripture (1 Corinthians 2:13). That way, we do not miss any details of the entire context of the issue. In the four versions of the gospel, Matthew, Mark, Luke and John, one of these men picked up on details of Jesus' teachings that the other men missed. That is why there are four different men's versions of the gospel, so we do not miss any vital details of Jesus' teachings.

Matthew 5:32 is one of the two scriptures that is almost point blank about marriage after a divorce. But naïve people twist this scripture around so that it agrees with the other vague scriptures of this issue, and makes God say what they want to hear Him say, to legitimize their reasons to get divorced. But this appears to be the most precise quote of Jesus, than in the other gospels, of why there is to be no remarriage of someone who is divorced, compared to Matthew 19:9.

To elaborate on Matthew 5:32, most people will put this scripture aside, in its exactness, or twist the words to that it agrees with the vagueness of Matthew 19:9, and other vague scriptures, regarding this alleged excusable reason for divorce.

To examine Matthew 5:32, there are actually two separate statements in this scripture.

First, "Whoever divorces his wife for any reason, except sexual immorality, causes her to commit adultery."

Second, "Whoever marries a woman who is divorced commits adultery." No exceptions are in this statement. It is the first statement that we need to dissect and examine. It is up to you to agree with my interpretation, but what I see, this most precise teaching about divorce and remarriage is:

Whoever divorces his wife causes her to commit adultery, when her human desires for a man in her life are refurbished, unless she had already been cheating on her husband before he divorced her. If she has been a faithful wife when her husband divorces her, the husband is partly responsible for her committing adultery, whether the adultery is through fornication or through what would be considered an adulterous marriage to a second man.

But if the wife has already been unfaithful to her husband, being involved with someone other than her husband, while still being married to the original husband, the original husband does not cause her to commit adultery when he divorces her, because she has already been committing adultery.

In short, and to rephrase Matthew 5:32, if a husband divorces his wife for any reason, except sexual immorality, he is responsible for his wife committing adultery when she gets lonely. And whoever marries a divorced woman commits adultery. But there are no permissible exceptions for divorce in this scripture.

So, let's answer this question: Why do I believe my interpretation is right, and why would God not allow any reasons or exceptions for divorce? The answer is Malachi 2:16: "For the Lord God of Israel says that he hates divorce, for it covers ones garment with violence."—God hates divorce, <u>No Exceptions</u>.

Marriages and divorces (unfortunately) take place regularly. Also, unfortunately, couples decide to commit only after they discover the female partner is pregnant. The opposite is what should be true. If a man and woman love each other to decide to have sex, thinking there is no way she will get pregnant, than they should love each other to where they are willing to make their love official and legitimate in the eyes of God and the law and get married.

I wonder how many children bear the weight of a form of guilt and low self esteem, because their parents are not married or only got married after said children were conceived.

And what about the marriages and divorces of people who are classified as celebrities? Understandably, all classes of people make mistakes. Celebrities are always made to be public examples. Their first marriage ends in divorce, but their second marriage turns out to be the right one.

But, then there are the "puppies." 'Puppy Love.' The term 'puppy love' is literally about dogs. A male and female dog are attracted to each other; the male gets the female pregnant; but neither necessarily commit to each other. That is the kind of so-called love we see in Hollywood, and other types of celebrity atmospheres. They are dogs; habitual marriers and divorcers who have absolutely no understanding to what the God-founded institute of marriage is all about. A life time commitment between one man and one woman, 'till death do we part.'

Some people get married a short time after meeting each other and have a good marriage (Paul and Linda McCartney). And some people wait for years. Other people are too worried about time, to trust Gods' timing. There are people who need to be concerned about Gods' will rather than human nature.

The reason God designed marriage as a strict institution is because earthly, heterosexual marriages are supposed to be an illustration of the eternal marriage of God and His bride; His people, the Church.

(In Jeremiah chapter 3 through chapter 4, verse 2, Gods people committed spiritual adultery. And yet, God pleaded with His people, "Return to me, for I am married to you." God did not completely divorce Himself from His people; He pleaded with His people to return to Him, and to abandon the other gods they went away to worship.)

(And, we can't build God's kingdom through homosexuality, because procreation is not possible with homosexuals. Hence, homosexuality is a sin.)

How Old is the Universe?

Scientists have estimated the universe to be billions of years old. Christian scholars, on the other hand, have estimated it to be about 6000 years old. Who is right? Obviously, the evolutionists will agree with the secular scientists. I spoke briefly with a Rabbi about this topic. The Rabbi said that paleontologists use fossils to estimate the age of the universe. But I said that fossils have no birth certificates. He immediately agreed.

As a challenge to the evolutionists and their doctrine of the big bang tale let us try using the Bible.

In our current year, we use the term A.D., which means Anno Domini, the year of our Lord. It has been about 2000 years since Jesus was on Earth.

Next we go to three books of the Bible that list genealogies. Matthew lists genealogies of Jesus back to Abraham. But Luke lists Jesus genealogies all the way back to Adam, the first human. And remember that Joseph was Jesus' step-father. God is Jesus' real father, in a Biblical sense.

But there is another book in the Bible very essential to estimating the age of the universe, the Chronicles. 1 Chronicles 1:1–28 list Adam to Isaac, but there is one more book to look at, Genesis 5:1–32. This chapter also lists Jesus' adopted ancestors, but one important feature in this book is the ages of each ancestor, when they begot the next descendant leading up to Jesus. The list is as follows:

Adam was 130 years old when he begot Seth; Seth was 105 years old when he begot Enosh; Enosh was 90 when he begot Cainan; Cainan, 70, Mahalaleel, 65, Jared, 162, Enoch, 65, Methuselah, 187, Lamech, 182 and Noah was 500 years old when he begot Shem. And this is where the list of ages stops.

Now let us do some math: 1,556 years from Adam to Shem, 11 generations. 2008 years from Jesus to today. Sixty-five generations between Shem and Jesus, with no ages listed. 2005 + 1556 = 3561 years. Christian scholars estimation of 6000 years: 6000 − 3561 = 2439 years left, with 65 generations with no ages listed: 65 + 11 = 76 generations between Adam and Jesus.

Question: How many generations would it take to come up with 1,000,000 (one million) years? How many generations have existed between Jesus and today? Since Jesus' half-brother? From a birds eye view, to me, it looks like not enough generations have existed to add up to 1,000,000 years, aside from billions of years.

But there is another source of information to look at— The Jewish New Year, also called Rosh Hashanah. Christians and Jews both believe in the same God, Jehovah, Yhwh, but the Jews generally have not come to accept that Jesus is the Messiah, God in the flesh and that is the limit to our differences.

As I was visiting the Rabbi, I looked into a book about the Jewish New Year, wondering what the focal point of Rosh Hashanah is? I had a guess and my guess was right. Rosh Hashanah is the anniversary of the creation of the universe. In the current time frame, the Jewish year is about 5765, in the Spring of A.D. 2005. This comes quite close to the Christian scholars estimation of 6000 years. In fact, the Jewish calendar is probably 99.89% more accurate than any Christian scholars' calculations, and realistic than the uneducated guesses of the evolutionists.

Judging

We all have built-in knowledge of right and wrong—sin and non-sin. Some theologians say it is pride that causes us to pass judgment when we ourselves commit our own sins. But if we want to try to help someone who is blinded by their own mistakes, we must first be humble enough to recognize and confess our own imperfection to the person we are trying to help, to avoid giving the image of being an outright hypocrite.

A lady in a restaurant told me an older man came in for a sandwich. He told the lady to step back for a moment and he made a complimentary, comment about part of her anatomy. She told me he was a pervert.

But recently, this same lady disclosed that she had a baby with some guy she was not married to. So, from Biblical standards, she is also perverted. So she has no room to judge.

More often times, we pass judgment, being ignorant and forgetful of our own mistakes. We should be comparing ourselves to God and not to each other.

Jesus said, "First, pull the plank out of you own eye; then you will see clearly to pull the spec out of your neighbors eye." Matthew 7:1–5; Luke 6:41–42.

The Biblical definition of 'grace' is 'God's unmerited favor' toward us. We shouldn't pass condemning judgement on others, but should be showing God's grace, to help the "blind" to see. And we shouldn't be quick to judge because we could discover that God IS at work in a person, transforming their life.

So take time to get to know your acquaintance before deciding what to say.

Marriage/Common Law Marriage/ Homosexuality

In these latter days, marriage is not being taken as seriously as it should be, from a Godly perspective. Divorce and adultery/fornication are all around us. A prime example is what we see reported in Hollywood, and occasionally in Washington D.C., (not to mention the Hollywood producers that promote it, along with other sins they promote.) This especially holds true in the homosexual rebellion.

People are too foolish to understand Gods plan for marriage, because it is an illustration of the upcoming eternal marriage of God and His people, the Church; one man, one woman committed for life, till death do they part.

This commitment is not only to each other, but it is also a commitment to God. And as you study the topics of Marriage, Adultery, Divorce, (and Homosexuality,) you will learn that God calls sex out of marriage, with a spouse, adultery and/or fornication.

If we are not sure what may lie ahead in the future for a married life, the advice to men and women is to pray and allow the Holy Spirit to guide you. (Christian counseling would also be helpful.)

In regard to homosexuals, politicians who claim to be Christians wimp out, trying to be politically correct, by promoting, what they call "traditional" marriage, between one man and one woman. But the word "traditional" is a shallow term. If these Christian politicians want to take a bold stand for God, they should describe marriage as "Godly" or "God-designed"; one man, one woman. Homosexual marriages have NO Godly moral, potential, and it is a sin worthy of death. (Leviticus 18:22; Leviticus 20:13.)

People	Sin
Negro	Homosexual
Caucasian	Murder
Hispanic	Stealing
German	Adultery
Polish	Bullying
Hom~~o~~sexual	

Regarding common law marriage, many people say that marriage is just a piece of paper. This vagueness has expanded into the sinful realm of homosexuality. First came heterosexual couples deciding to just live together without getting married, but enjoying the sexual indulgences of marriage (adultery/fornication.) (But now, homosexual couples want the same legal benefits as legitimate, heterosexual married couples have.)

Common law marriage says, if a man and a woman live together for at least 24 hours, or 7 years, they are married. So, they have to live in a state of adultery before they're declared married. But they have no legal documentation to legitimize this marriage.

Marriage is more than a piece of paper. It is God's law. And we must recognize that all earthly laws have a Godly origin.

In Gods kingdom, God is referred to as the "husband." God's people are the "bride"; Revelation 21:1–2, Revelation 21:9. In this marriage of God and His kingdom, God gives them a new name; Revelation 2:17, Isaiah 62:1–2. In Isaiah, the bride is described as being given a new name. This is where the Biblical rite of the wife taking on her husband's name comes from. (From Miss to Misses; Mrs.) This name change is documented by an earthly law marriage certificate. Again, this is to illustrate the marriage of God and His kingdom.

Homosexuals are not Biblically qualified to be married, because God assigned (designed) men to be the husbands and women to be the wives. (Genesis 2:21–24; Genesis 9:1; Leviticus 18:22; Leviticus 20:13; Genesis 18:16–19:29.) (Part of the reason is to procreate and multiply the human race. Homosexual couples can not physically procreate. They can only imitate by adopting.)

The issue nowadays is secularists, atheists, and modern alleged Christians say that the government has no business declaring who is married and who is not, as documented on a legal marriage certificate, which grants the wife the Biblical rite of taking on her husbands last name.

In decades past, one example was when the mail was delivered. If a piece of mail was addressed to the wife, it would read either with the wife's first name, or the husbands first name; I.E. Mrs. Jane Doe or Mrs. John Doe.

In regard to a piece of paper, marriage is a legal contract, not just emotional or mental bonding.

In Deuteronomy 24:1–4, Moses instructed God's people, that if a husband puts away his wife, he was to hand her a certificate, or a bill, of divorce. Why was this? What is a certificate for? To prove the existence of a divorce.

<u>If you need a document to prove divorce, implicitly, you need a document to prove marriage.</u> This is because (we have to be reminded) in God-fearing times, the government was recognized to be ordained by God (Romans 13:1,) and are

inseparable, contrary to what todays generation is trying to do in separating God from government (Psalms 2; Luke 19:27)

(Also, see "Separation of Church and State.")

Remember; marriage is not a mental or emotional bond with a person; it is a legal establishment, between one man and one woman. God ordained it that way. (Deuteronomy 24:1–4; Jeremiah 3:6–4:4; Mark 10:1–9; John 2:1.)

Murder

There was a movie called "West Side Story". It was about two racial gangs at odds with each other. But a man from one group and a lady from the other group fell in love.

Near the end of the movie, three people were killed. One was the man who was in love with the woman from the other group. The woman took the gun, pointed it at both rival groups and implicitly asked 'Why?'

In her anger and grief, she yelled at both gangs and said, "You don't kill with bullets and guns!! You kill with hate!! Well, I can kill too, because now I have hate!!!!

Why did God allow our genealogical appearances to separate? Naturally, to conform to our environmental surroundings, but this is superficial. Ultimately, probably to test us in the second greatest commandment.

We are all subject to being prejudice against someones outward appearance, speech, accent, age, disability, or whatever seems to bother us. But as many mothers would say, 'It's what's inside that counts.'

In three separate situations I was swept off my feet by three ladies, all of different races. The cause of my emotional rush was their personalities. Their outward appearances were no issue.

The psyche is an invisible part of us we all have, also known as the soul. Just as a person's appearance can affect the superficial part of our soul, the surface, a person's personality can affect the inner part of our soul, regardless of their outward appearance, including weight and complexion. But you have to experience what I am talking about to understand what I am talking about.

Regarding this movie, saying we kill with hate, Jesus said something more explicit:

Matthew 5:21–22, "You have heard it said 'You shall not murder,' and whoever murders shall be in danger of judgment. But I say to you, that whoever is angry against his brother without a cause shall be in danger of THE judgment."

With all of the homicides we hear about, a normal and typical reaction would be, "I don't understand why," and, "it doesn't make any sense."

Besides the scripture reference in James 4:1–3, another answer to simplify what we would like to know is, growing up surrounded by and seeing hatred all around us. People simply are full of insatiable, anger, hatred and/or jealousy, and/or stupidity. And we can observe it, and involuntarily learn it.

Prophesies of the Last Days

We are seeing it all around us, AIDS coming out in the 20ᵗʰ century, homosexuals coming out of the closet and taking a stand and now homosexual unions becoming legal; the increasing number of earth tremors and other natural disasters becoming more destructive; blood shed has increased to where traditional laws of war (Geneva Convention) no longer apply; teenagers committing murder; abuse and neglect of children and the elderly.

And people are asking, with regard to the Creator of the universe, 'Where is God in all of this?' Why has God allowed things to become so out of control? If God is a loving God, why has he allowed so much violence to come into the world?

There are two possibilities. First, from a birds eye view, we see sin increasing in the world, including in the Christian community. One example, in pornography, Christians have been known to purchase the adulterous material. In one interview, a pornographic model made reference to her church. (!)(?)

Also, homosexuals are getting the recognition they have been demanding. The terms 'gay' and 'queer' were used as words to make fun of homosexuals, but now the terms gay, queer and lesbian have been officially adopted as legal accepted titles to mistakenly legitimize their filthy, sinful life style.

The word 'gay' originally meant joyful. But lets not fool ourselves; homosexuals are not "gays," they are homosexuals. And if you'll look in the topic of Homosexuality, you will see that God has condemned this practice as a sin worthy of death.

God's will is for people to increase in number on the earth. So he created, in the laws of nature, males and females to have sexual relations (in the institution of marriage) in order to accomplish this. God is the author of all laws, moral, natural and scientific. God does not allow homosexuality to be an option or alternative life style. God says homosexuality is a sin. (Romans 1:18–22)

And homosexuality has expanded. For several years, there has been a homosexual in Congress. But now, there are churches, in their Biblical stupidity, who are appointing homosexuals as priests, deacons, choir directors and other church elders. (See "Requirements for Church Elders")

In short, sin is expanding all over the world. Back in Isaiah 30:9, God says, "This is a rebellious people; children will not listen to the law of the Lord. And in 2 Chronicles 7:14, God says, "If my people will humble themselves, and pray, and seek my face, and turn from their wicked ways, then I will hear from Heaven, and will forgive their sin, and will heal their land." (2nd Corinthians 6:14–18; Revelation 18.)

Another sin that is at epidemic proportions is divorce. Wedding vows at ceremonies have lost their meaning, they are just words. One reason is people are just in too much of a hurry to tie the knot, without spending enough quantity of time, as well as quality of time courting.

So, one possibility for God allowing all of the physical and social destruction and violent deaths is Christians allowing sin to become part of their life style. (Romans 1:18–22)

An example of 2 Chronicles 7:14 is the book of Jonah. The city of Nineveh was filled with sin. But because God used Jonah to warn the people of God's threatening judgment, the entire city, from the king to the peasants repented. (Romans 1:21–22)

On the other hand, the second possibility for the decline in our society—when we look into what Jesus described as signs of the end times, the unwanted things that are happening, are happening because Jesus said they would happen prior to his return and judgment day.

Why should these be the types of signs? Simply because this is God's will. Any further questions will have to be asked to God after we are all brought to Heaven. But the only reason I can think of is that this is the way God is using to get glory for himself. And since he is the Supreme Being, and the Creator of the universe, he has every right to get his glory anyway he chooses.

So, you see, things in the world are out of control, God is still in control. S.R.N. news service on September 10, 2005, said that the European nations, right up to the government level, are now living in a post-Christian era. And observing what we see around the United States, the United States is heading in that direction also.

So it looks to me like Judgment Day could be very well closer than we think. We will all stand before God. Romans 14:12; Revelation 20:12; Psalms 80.

The National Tabloid

Biblical Prophesy Fulfilled!

We have all caught a glimpse of the illegitimate tabloids, occasionally having a headline about alleged Bible prophesy. Well, a local newspaper got my attention about one prophesy that definitely was fulfilled! And it was brought to my attention by the local Lancaster newspaper; not an illegitimate tabloid.

In Revelation 6:5–6, this money, called a 'denarius' was evaluated as about $20 back in 1985. But essentially is valued as a days worth of employers wages.

On March 15, 2008, the Associated Press reported that wheat, as mentioned in this reference of Revelation, historically trades at $3 to $7 a bushel; apparently what the Bible means by a 'measure.' But in this article, on the date in question, wheat and its byproducts (bread, bagels, rolls, etc.) was reported to cost $18 a bushel, and ran up to $24 in the previous February.

That is explicit and exact Bible prophesy occurring before our eyes, <u>almost unlike any other.</u> Several months ago, a then-fellow employee, who now works at the mall, said to me, "I know the Bible talks about these things happening; but I STILL don't believe it has anything to do with it." (The Bible) That is an expression of explicit blindness, as it could ever be.

And even when I show this to some fellow Christians who pass my way, some seem to brush it off.

But even up to today, in May of 2011, this financial turmoil covers more than just wheat.

Add that to a possibility of a one-world government threat. Should we be concerned? Yes, and no. If we look at Hebrews, Chapter 11, the writer of Hebrews teaches that the faithful people of the past never lived long enough on Earth to receive Gods promises, but did see the promises afar off, were assured of them.

In the same way, in this threat of a one-world government, it has been researched and taught by other theologians that, this one-world government will not be established until after Gods people are taken up into Heaven. So, we can say that these events, like the Euro-dollar and the financial "collapse by design" concept, are a small prelude to what will happen after our rapture.

Regarding the skeptics, they'll say that these natural disasters and wars have been going on for centuries, and still no Judgement Day, (2 Peter 3.) But, what I have realized is that this article about the wheat prices is not something that's been going on for centuries. In the 20th century alone, I've heard about and witnessed climbing prices. My father once told me he used to pay 5¢ for a loaf of bread. When I was a child, the first price of a first-class postage stamp (I remember) was 6¢; I paid 10¢ for a candy bar, and 20¢ for a 12 ounce soda. On a news report in 1973, the reporter said, "It's 1973; gasoline is 36¢ a gallon." My mother used to pull up to the gas pump and order $1 worth of gas.

But, this article about the wheat prices—<u>this is the *first*</u>

report of its kind, in the history of the world, coinciding with Revelation 6:5–6; the cost of wheat rising to the equivalent of a days worth of employers wages. (Lancasteronline.com; Intelligencer Journal/New Era, page A2, "Soaring Wheat Prices"; Mar. 15, 2008; Betsy Blaney, Associated Press)

Of all the other reports, I think this is the most conspicuous reported mile-post showing the way to Judgement Day.

Money/Wealth/Greed

1 Timothy 6:10, KJV, "For the love of money is the root of all evil, which while some have coveted after, they have erred from the faith, and pierced themselves through with many sorrows." (Divorce, etc.)

NKJV, "For the love of money is the root of all [kinds] of evil, for which some have strayed from the faith in their greediness and pierced themselves through with many sorrows."

NAS, "For the love of money is the root of all sorts of evil and some, by longing for it, have wandered away from the faith, and pierced themselves with many a pang."

NIV, "For the love of money is a root of all kinds of evil. Some people eager for money have wandered from the faith and pierced themselves with many griefs." (Divorce, etc.)

These are all of the translations of the Bible in my personal "library." I am not sure if it was a misquote, but I have heard some quoting the Bible as saying "Money is the root of all evil. . . ." Rather than "the love of money"

Another man I met told me about another mans studious translation, from the ancient languages, 'Evil revolves around money."

This issue was brought to my attention, more vividly today. I pondered how money has had its part in corrupting peoples minds, right down to destroying peoples lives. Married couples (heterosexual) have been known to get divorced because they either have too much money, or not enough, including runaway spending.

In my personal comparison of these four Bible translations, I agree with parts of each one.

In an attempt to not point the finger, I thought about at least one young lady who has made so much money in her celebrity career, that she does not know what to do with most of it, like so many wealthy people, who are out of control. So, she bought herself an expensive car, to her liking, a mansion, probably a bunch of jewelry, etc. etc.

And, with some of that surplus she buys alcoholic drinks and maybe illegal drugs (?) and finally, as a result of her out-of-control and Godless life style, loses custody of her children to their father, who, in Gods law, is still married to her.

Although Jesus told us not to pass judgment on each other there is a part of our souls that is made to judge, discern and weigh the facts as well as the fictions.

Many people would look at this woman's performances and say, "She's out of control, what is her problem?" Her problem, as well as a lot of people like her, is her money and/or the love and pursuit of money and a lack of maturity to know how to handle it.

Excessive money can cause people to became so self-sufficient, that as the Bible evidently says, they wander astray from their faith in God. This wandering from faith in God does not necessarily result in prodigal living, but evidently can result in one becoming so dilutionally self-sufficient, that God is expelled out of ones life, and wealth becomes their god.

Satan became self sufficient, as the angel, Lucifer, who was the glorious looking angel, of the entire legion. (Ones physical appearance can also cause one to become his or her own god.) He became to proud and arrogant, that he declared, "I will ascend into Heaven; I will exalt my throne above the stars of God; I will sit on the mount of the congregation; I will be like the Most High." (Isaiah 14:12–31; Ezekiel 28:1–19)

And, now, look at how many celebrities are ignorantly taking on this role of being a god, either by their physical appearance or their money; I.E., the singers, the actors, sports figures, super models, politicians. Some have had their livelihood destroyed or have died at a comparatively young age.

Wealth is a blessing from God, but if not dealt with and managed it can cause the end of it's owners life. (Matthew 6:19–21)

What Christmas is All About;
A.K.A., the Gospel

1. Genesis 1:1–27
2. Genesis 3:1–19
3. Genesis 4:1–14A
4. Genesis 6:5–6
5. Exodus 20:1–17
6. Isaiah 29:13, (Matthew 15:8; Mark 7:6–7)
7. Romans 3:10–18; (Psalms 14:1–3; Psalms 53:1–3; Psalms 5:9; Psalms 140:3; Psalms 10:7; Ecclesiastes 7:20; Isaiah 59:7–8; Psalms 36:1
8. Jeremiah 6:20
9. Isaiah 1:11–13
10. 1 Samuel 15:22
11. Hosea 6:6; Matthew 9:13
12. Genesis 22:1–8
13. Isaiah 53:6
14. Romans 6:23
15. Isaiah 53:4–5
16. Romans 5:8
17. Hebrews 10:4
18. 1 John 4:9–10
19. Matthew 1:20–21
20. John 1:29
21. Matthew 11:28–29
22. John 3:16
23. Matthew 20:28
24. John 10:10B
25. Luke 19:10
26. John 3:17
27. John 12:47B
28. John 14:1–6

One of the Christmas carols that demonstrates what Christmas is all about, says,

"Hark! The herald angels sing,
Glory to the newborn king.
Peace on Earth, and mercy, mild;
God and sinners reconciled."

Sin separates us from God. Christ came into the world as the Supreme Atonement for our sins, provided by God, so that we can be reconciled to God.

One of the controversial Biblical phrases is "Peace on Earth." Isaiah 9:6 refers to Jesus as the "Prince of peace." But this is not talking about an anti-war peace. This is talking about a kind of truce between God and sinners; for sinners to repent of their evil life styles, and be reconciled to God. (Ephesians 2:14–18; Colossians 1:19–23)